C000051014

VAL HORSLER

Jack the Ripper

the national archives

First published in 2007 by
The National Archives
Kew, Richmond
Surrey, TW9 4DU, UK

www.nationalarchives.gov.uk

The National Archives
brings together the Public Record Office,
Historical Manuscripts Commission,
Office of Public Sector Information
and Her Majesty's Stationery Office.

© Val Horsler 2007

The right of Val Horsler to be identified as
the Author of this work has been asserted by her in accordance
with the Copyright, Designs and Patents Act 1988.

All rights reserved. No part of this publication may be reproduced,
stored in a retrieval system or transmitted, in any form or by any means,
electronic, mechanical, photocopying, recording or otherwise without
the prior permission of both the copyright holder and the above publisher.

A catalogue card for this book is available from the British Library.

ISBN 978 1 905615 14 8

Cover illustration: discovery of the final
Whitechapel murder in 1891 (Roger-Viollet/Topfoto)
Cover design by Goldust Design
Page design and typesetting by Ken Wilson | point 918
Picture research by Gwen Campbell
Printed in Germany by
Bercker Graphischer Betrieb GmbH & Co

Contents

———

Introduction:
The Whitechapel Killings · *5*

One · The First Murders · *18*

Two · A Maniac at Large · *32*

Three · The Final Act? · *53*

Four · Hunted and Hunters · *75*

Five · The Ripper Legend · *94*

Sources & Reading · *109*

Index · *111*

The murderer must have been a man of physical strength &
of great coolness & daring ... subject to periodical attacks of
homicidal & erotic mania.

... [He] is quite likely to be a quiet inoffensive looking man
probably middle aged and neatly and respectably dressed.
I think he must be in the habit of wearing a cloak or overcoat
or he could hardly have escaped notice in the streets if the
blood on his hands or clothes were visible.

... He is possibly living among respectable persons who have
some knowledge of his character and habits and who may have
grounds for suspicion that he is not quite right in his mind at
times.

Dr Thomas Bond, police surgeon

The Whitechapel Killings

By 15 October 1888 five women had been viciously murdered and mutilated in the wretched back streets of London's East End. The killer had not been caught, but he had a name, 'Jack the Ripper'—the signature on a number of letters received by the police and the press, taunting them for their failure to catch him and promising further horrors. On that mid-October day, two weeks had passed since the last murders, and press coverage had died down somewhat. But throughout the country hysteria was bubbling under the surface, as a letter published that day in *The Times* illustrates:

> Two days ago I was approached by a party of seven stout collier lads, who rudely demanded my name, which, of course, I refused to give. 'Then you are Jack the Ripper, and you will come along with us to the police…'. Now, I do not object to adventures, even in the decline of life; nor do I much blame my antagonists, whether their motive were righteous indignation, or, as is more likely, the hope of reward. But I think them guilty of a serious and even dangerous error of judgement in not

distinguishing between the appearance of Jack the Ripper and
that of your obedient servant, An Elderly Gentleman.

The elderly gentleman was Arthur Munby, civil servant, diarist
and poet, who was several hundred miles away from London
visiting his wife in Hadley, Shropshire. Munby's experience was
not unusual. The recent killings meant that solitary men every-
where were objects of suspicion, whether they were furtive-
looking tramps or conformed to one of the popular conceptions
of Jack the Ripper as a well-educated, well-dressed member of
the decadent upper classes. The two weeks without a murder
had aroused the fear that Jack might have left London and was
about to continue his ghastly work elsewhere — the local press
in cities like Manchester and Newcastle reported the dread
that gripped their young women, and national and even international newspapers continued to feed sensation-seekers with
the lurid details of the Whitechapel murders.

This press frenzy was a new phenomenon. As well as creating a climate of fear and suspicion it made the crimes a *cause
célèbre*, both at the time and to the present day. In the autumn
of 1888 crowds flocked from all over London to the murder
scenes in Whitechapel. Those fortunate enough to live next
door to the yard in Hanbury Street where Annie Chapman had
been so viciously butchered could charge voyeurs good money
to view the spot. Now, almost 120 years later, the much-changed
Ripper crime scenes remain a tourist draw. The graves of the
victims, where they are known, are marked with heritage trail

plaques and are often covered with tributes left by visitors. Scores of books have been published, and websites devoted to the murders receive thousands of hits. And more than anything else, attempts to put a name to this mysterious murderer who was not caught and has never been unmasked are seemingly unending.

Yet it is almost certain that the identity of Jack the Ripper will never be decisively known. He has become the bogeyman of the late-Victorian period in London's East End, despite the fact that the murders most justifiably laid at his door took place over just four months from August to November 1888. In fact, he was probably just one of a number of 'Whitechapel murderers' responsible for the unsolved violent deaths of 11 women between April 1888 and February 1891. Opinion is still divided about how many of those were true Ripper victims, though the consensus is that he certainly killed four and possibly six. Those generally accepted as his victims—dubbed the 'canonical five'— are Mary Ann Nichols, Annie Chapman, Elizabeth Stride, Catherine Eddowes and Mary Jane Kelly, though some researchers raise a doubt about Elizabeth Stride because her body, unlike the other four, was not mutilated. Despite his reputation as the archetypal serial killer, therefore, the Ripper probably operated only over a very short period and other men were responsible for the other deaths.

The horrific nature of the injuries inflicted on the victims might be enough to explain the continuing fascination with the

Ripper crimes. The police and medical reports make unsettling reading, and the murders were fully reported in all their gory detail in the press of the time. But even that killing spree might have faded away into the fog of the late nineteenth century if it had not been for the name the murderer apparently gave himself.

'Jack the Ripper' is not perhaps the most creative name for a knifeman. But it instantly caught the public's imagination. The publication in the press of what is known as the 'Dear Boss' letter in early October 1888—the first to bear the Ripper signature—was the catalyst for a flood of hoax missives signed with that name. The letters continued through 1889, trickling on until 1891, while another letter received in 1896 threatened further murders. The name stuck, and there is an undoubted frisson in the idea that one or more of these missives, which are now held at the National Archives and can be viewed on microfilm, may have come from the pen of the murderer. Yet the late-Victorian police were convinced (and modern researchers tend to agree) that the real murderer did not seek attention in this way, and that the thick file of letters says more about the vagaries of human nature than it does about the crimes. The one letter regarded as possibly authentic—that sent to George Lusk along with a piece of human kidney (see p. 61)—was not signed 'Jack the Ripper'. It is tantalizing enough that we are denied the name of the murderer, but almost equally frustrating that we will also never know who coined the world-famous Ripper name.

The documentary record itself is evidence of the Ripper's continued hold on the public imagination. The National Archives has been forced to lock away the original material because of pilfering over the years—and some of the iconic material in the case only re-emerged in 1987, almost a century after the murders, when an anonymous packet with a Croydon postmark was received at Scotland Yard. It contained, among other papers, the original of the 'Dear Boss' letter and the post-mortem report on the last victim. The envelope was fingerprinted and enquiries were made, but its sender was never discovered. It is assumed that the material was removed by an officer from the police archives in the early twentieth century, as a souvenir of this and other cases (there was also some Crippen material, for example), and that his conscience-stricken descendants decided to return it anonymously.

More recently still, in December 2000, speculation flared again when Ripper authority Donald Rumbelow gave the Metropolitan Police what is known as the 'Openshaw letter'. This was another Jack the Ripper missive sent in late October 1888 to Thomas Openshaw, the curator of the pathological museum at the London Hospital who examined the kidney sent to George Lusk. The 'Lusk letter' itself is missing from the archives, and is available now only in facsimile, but the link between it and this latest addition to public record—now held at the National Archives—is inextricable. You might wonder, what else is out there?

LONDON'S SLUM LIFE

The Ripper case was, and still is, public property. Perhaps this is because the murders were among the first to reach a wide audience via the growing power of the press, which seized on the crimes not just to sell newspapers but for political and sociological ends too. Some editors castigated the Home Secretary and the police for the lack of progress in apprehending the killer, while others refused to blame them for their failure to catch a man of extreme boldness who worked furtively and alone. And as the horrors grew, so did the reporting of them; no punches were pulled in the vivid, detailed, almost bloodthirsty press accounts of the crimes. Their revelations about living conditions in Whitechapel aroused feelings of both disgust and sympathy, as well as vicarious fascination with the darker side of urban life. Many newspaper reports refused to condemn the victims as the vicious dregs of society that the word 'prostitute' might suggest, while the jury foreman at one of the inquests announced that he would be willing to put up a £25 reward since 'these poor people have souls like everyone else'. And the report in the 10 November 1888 edition of *The Times* included a moving account of local reaction to Mary Jane Kelly's murder:

> The news that the body was about to be removed caused a
> great rush of people from the courts running out of Dorset
> Street, and there was a determined effort to break the police
> cordon at the Commercial Street end. The crowd, which

pressed round the van, was of the humblest class, but the demeanour of the poor people was all that could be described. Ragged caps were doffed and slatternly-looking women shed tears as the shell [coffin], covered with a ragged-looking cloth, was placed in the van.

It is perhaps the little facts that emerge from the surviving documents and press reports that are most telling about conditions in the late-Victorian slums of east London. A poignant reminder of the prevailing poverty and hand-to-mouth way of life is the remark by Mary Ann Nichols to another woman at 2.30 am on the night she was killed that she was trying to earn 4d (four pence—under 2p in today's money) to pay for her bed for the night, having been turned away from her lodging house because she was penniless. Contrast this with another fact revealed by the Ripper material—the price of a postage stamp at the time, which was 1d or ½d. Of course the postal service of 120 years ago was expensive, but even so, the relative costs of a stamp and a bed for the night are pointed reminders of the deep divide between rich and poor. As John Kelly, Catherine Eddowes' companion, testified at her inquest:

We had been unfortunate at the hop-picking and had no money. On Thursday night we both slept in the casual ward [where they got a bed and food in return for work]. On the Friday I earned 6d at a job, and I said, 'Here, Kate, you take 4d and go to the lodging-house and I will go to Mile End,' but she said, 'No, you go and have a bed and I will go to the casual ward…'

On other occasions, as he testified, if they had no money to pay
for a bed they were reduced to walking the streets all night.

The inquest records (all in HO 144/221/A49301C) also show, however, that those living in this way were often inclined to spend
any available money on drink. Most of the Ripper's victims
were drunk when they died, and drinking problems caused several of them to be thrown out by their husbands. Amelia
Palmer, a resident of the lodging house where Annie Chapman
lived, testified that she

> was a very industrious woman when she was sober. I have seen
> her often the worse for drink. She could not take much without
> making her drunk. She had been living a very irregular life
> during the whole time that I have known her … [although she]
> was a very respectable woman, and never used bad language.

And John Kelly revealed that he and Eddowes pawned his
boots for 2s 6d (12½p) and spent the money on drink and food;
according to Kelly, she went into the pawnshop to pawn the
boots as 'I stood in the doorway in my bare feet.' On the night
she was murdered, a drunken Eddowes was locked up in a police
cell until she sobered up enough in the early hours to be
released—as it happened, into the path of her killer.

In the language of the time, the Ripper's victims were
'unfortunates': women whose main way of earning money was
to work as prostitutes in the streets, lifting their skirts to passing men in return for a few pence. Such women were the cheap-
est of those working in the trade. Of the six women murdered

between August and November 1888 only one had a room to which she could take her client; the others were all murdered in the streets or, in Martha Tabram's case, in the public stairwell of a common lodging house. An October 1888 police report to the Home Office (MEPO 3/141) details over 200 of those lodging houses 'naturally frequented by prostitutes, thieves and tramps as there is nowhere else for them to go, and no law to prevent their congregating there'. These lodgings provided a base for women who plied their trade casually, women who were among the 'about 1200 prostitutes, mostly of a very low condition' described in the report.

Some residents of the East End deplored the reputation of the place. A letter to *The Times* of 23 July 1889 from Samuel Barnett, Vicar of St Jude's, Whitechapel, indicates as much, though his sentiments also betray a rather unchristian attempt to lay the blame for the murders firmly on the wretched victims:

The record tells of rows in which stabbing is common, but on which the police are able to get no charges; of fights between women stripped to the waist, of which boys and children are spectators; of the protection afforded to thieves, and of such things as could only occur where opinion favours vice. The district in which all this happens is comparatively small; it forms, indeed, a black spot ... in the midst of a neighbourhood which in no way deserves the reputation for ill conduct. A district so limited might be easily dealt with, and its reform is more important than even the capture of a murderer, who would have no victims if they were not prepared by degradation.

The Home Office and police response to this letter (HO 144/220/ A49301) agreed that 'vice of a low and degraded type is only too visible in Whitechapel' and that

> to anyone who will take a walk late at night in the district where the recent atrocities have been committed, the only wonder is that his operations have been so restricted. There is no lack of victims ready to his hand, for scores of these unfortunate women may be seen any night muddled with drink in the streets and alleys, perfectly reckless as to their safety, and only anxious to meet with anyone who will help them in plying their miserable trade.

However, it also commented that 'Brawling and fighting does and will take place amongst the low class of persons to be found in Whitechapel, but not nearly to such an extent as might be expected and is generally believed by persons non resident in the district.' And there was also a dig at Barnett's nimbyism: 'I pointed out to Mr Barnett that by clearing the neighbourhood he mentions, the persons at present there would be driven into the adjoining parishes which would naturally cause discontent, but he appears to think every one should clear his own house without regard to his neighbours.'

Police reports, inquest statements, newspaper articles—all help to paint a vivid picture of life, and particularly nightlife, in the East End of London in 1888–9. It was both a dingy, ill-lit neighbourhood, with many shadowy corners where dark deeds could go unnoticed, and a lively community, with much coming and going at all hours of the day and night (see plate 1). Shops were open late, as is clear from the statements of several witnesses who testified that they were on the streets in the early hours on their way to buy their supper at local chandlers. Matthew Packer, a greengrocer and a witness in the Stride case, believed that he might have sold grapes at 11.45 pm to a suspicious-looking man who, he thought, might have been with the victim. Lodging houses kept their doors open until 2 am, and nightwatchmen and the police patrolled regularly all night. Pubs and clubs closed late and work started early. John Reeves found Martha Tabram's body at 4.45 am as he was leaving home to seek work, and James Kent, a witness at the inquest on Annie Chapman's death, was at work in Hanbury Street at 6.10 am on the Saturday morning when her body was found.

The evidence of another witness at that inquest shows how closely packed were the living conditions at 29 Hanbury Street, where Chapman was killed. Amelia Richardson testified:

I am a widow, and occupy half of the house... On the ground floor there are two rooms. Mrs Hardman occupies them with her son, aged sixteen. She uses the front room as a cats' meat shop... John Davies and his family tenant the third floor front, and Mrs Sarah Cox has the back room on the same floor. She is an old lady I keep out of charity. Mr Thompson and his wife, with an adopted little girl, have the front room on the second floor... Two unmarried sisters reside in the second floor back. They work at a cigar factory.

Gloom and fog dominate images of the Ripper's East End, yet the first murders took place in high summer, and it is on record that October 1888 was a warm, balmy month without the usual smogs. The streets were as ever the haunt of people from all over London seeking drink and drugs in what have become known as gin palaces and opium dens, as well as sex from the cheap prostitutes who were to become the Ripper's prey. Opium was easily available, and not at this time illegal; it was an ingredient in many patent medicines including those used to soothe fretful children. Those drawn to the East End ranged from Prince Eddy, Queen Victoria's oldest grandson and second in line to the throne—who went there to seek out the dangerous thrills of 'slumming it' among the poor and the degraded—to those like William Ewart Gladstone who sought to help or reform the local unfortunates. But it was also teeming with people on legitimate business: men enjoying the social life and intellectual stimulation of the socialist club in whose yard Elizabeth Stride was killed, and others walking through Mitre Square on their way home after an evening out with friends; women passing the time of day on their doorsteps with neighbours; people going home late or out early to the market.

Whitechapel, day and night, was a place of contrasts. Nowhere is this encapsulated more vividly than an article in the American journal, *Littell's Living Age*, dated 3 November 1888 and seeking to enthrall its readers with the atmosphere of Whitechapel in the wake of the murders:

> At all times one who strolls through this quarter of town, espe-
> cially by night, must feel that below his ken are the awful deeps
> of an ocean teeming with life, but enshrouded in impenetrable
> mystery. As he catches here and there a glimpse of a face under
> the flickering, uncertain light of a lamp he may get a momen-
> tary shuddering sense of what humanity may sink to when life
> is lived apart from sweet, health-giving influences...

Rife with vice, drugs, crime and depravity it may have been, but
there was a vibrancy to East End life, and safety in numbers on
the teeming streets:

> It is a relief to work one's way back into the life and light of the
> great highway, with its flaunting shops, its piles of glowing
> fruit, its glittering jewellery, its steaming cook-shops, its flaring
> gin-palaces and noisy shows... Mr Charrington, whose great
> place stands out boldly on the Mile End highway a blaze of light
> and cheerfulness, thinks that people have more than ever
> thronged out of the dark and silent byways and back lanes into
> the broad pavement and into the glare of light thrown upon it
> by shops and public-houses and entertainments... But the nine
> days' wonder has passed, the effect of the shock has visibly
> subsided, and people are beginning to move freely again.

Not so, as it happens. Just a week after this article appeared in
print the Ripper was to strike again, more viciously than ever.

CHAPTER ONE

The First Murders

When Mary Ann 'Polly' Nichols was turned away from the common lodging house at 18 Thrawl Street, Spitalfields, where she had been living in a room with three other women for a few weeks, she laughed and said, 'I'll soon get my doss money; see what a jolly bonnet I've got now.' It was 1.40 am on the night of 31 August and she did not have the money to pay for her bed.

The bonnet that so pleased her was found lying beside her dead body only a few hours later and a few streets away in Buck's Row. Her throat had been viciously slashed and blood had pooled into the gutter next to her head. PC John Neil of the Metropolitan Police, who found her at 3.45 am (see plate 2), had walked along that road only half an hour before on his regular beat, and two other men had seen her lying there just before the policeman arrived. Whoever killed her had worked with quick and merciless violence.

The wounds to her throat were evidence of a sadistic thoroughness. But worse was to follow when the body was taken to the mortuary and Inspector Spratling, the officer on duty, examined it more closely. His report, written later that same day, is both measured and graphic (see plate 3). The document is damaged on its right edge, so some of the words are indecipherable or conjectural, but the overall message is clear:

> I found that she had been disembowelled, and at once sent to inform the doctor of it; he arrived quickly and on further examination stated that her throat had been cut from left to right… the windpipe, gullet and spinal cord being cut through, a bruise apparently of a thumb being on right lower jaw, also one on left cheek, the abdomen had been cut open from centre of bottom of ribs on right side, under pelvis to left of the stomach, there the wound was jagged, the omentium [*sic*] or coating of the stomach was also cut in several places, and there were small stabs on private parts, apparently done with a strong bladed knife… supposed to have been done by some left-handed person, death being instantaneous. (MEPO 3/140)

This was a bold, cold-blooded killer willing to take massive risks: of being caught in the act, of his hands and clothes being covered with the spurting blood of his victim, of her cries being overheard and of being challenged as he fled the scene. As the inquest evidence made clear, policemen were on patrol nearby and people were coming and going throughout the night. The two passers-by, Charles Andrew Cross and Robert Paul, who had seen her body lying on the pavement and thought she was either drunk or dead, had never met before. Both had independently walked down that street on their way home from work only a few minutes after the murder was committed.

When PC Neil found the body he was able to summon immediate help from two nearby policemen without, as he testified, even needing to blow his whistle. The killer must have had a very cool head indeed to have seized the brief moments when the street was deserted to approach his victim, kill her and inflict atrocities on her body.

PREVIOUS ACTS OF VIOLENCE

The viciousness of the murder and the audacity of the murderer immediately caught the attention of the press. Scenting a connection between this death and two earlier killings in Whitechapel that year, they began to speculate. Was there someone with a grudge against East End prostitutes, or even on a mission to rid the streets of women of ill repute? Was the ownership and use of a sharp knife evidence that the killer was a slaughterman? Or perhaps he was a medical man, someone educated and professionally qualified? Dr Llewellyn, who examined Nichols' body, was known to believe that the killer might have a knowledge of anatomy. The baying began.

The victims of those two earlier murders were Emma Smith, assaulted on 3 April 1888, and Martha Tabram, whose body was found in the early morning of 7 August. The Smith murder had excited little public disquiet, and the police were not even informed until two days after her death: attacks on prostitutes were common, and women who ventured into the ill-lit streets in the early hours were regarded as exposing themselves to foolish risk. Yet there were differences between Smith's murder and that of Nichols. Smith died of internal injuries the day after she was assaulted, but lived long enough to describe three attackers whose motive was robbery. It was a vicious assault: in addition to the fatal injuries she had bruises to her head and one of her ears was torn. But her death was caused by a blunt instrument. The weapon that mutilated Mary Ann Nichols, it seemed, was a knife, and according to medical reports one that was long, pointed and very sharp.

And it had also been with a knife—or knives, according to Dr Timothy Killeen who carried out the post-mortem—that Martha Tabram was brutally killed on 7 August. Her body was discovered lying in a pool of blood on the first floor landing of George Yard Buildings, George Yard, at 4.45 am. She was found by John Reeves, who was going out to seek work, and had probably been dead for two or three hours: a cab driver called Alfred Crow testified at the inquest that he had passed what may have been her body at 3.30 that morning as he was returning home but 'he took no notice, as he was accustomed to seeing people lying about there'. The post-mortem report revealed that the victim had 39 wounds on her body, mainly on her abdomen and at least one of them delivered, according to the doctor, by a bayonet or dagger. There was a single stab through the heart which would have been enough to cause death, but the doctor believed that most of the other wounds had been inflicted while she was alive—in other words while she was at least initially conscious of the attack. As the coroner remarked, the murderer 'must have been a perfect savage to inflict such a number of wounds on a defenceless woman in such a way'.

The inquest opened two days after the murder, on 9 August, by which time the victim had not been positively identified. When it resumed two weeks later on 23 August the police had been able to contact Tabram's husband. He recognized her as his former wife, from whom he 'had been separated for thirteen years, owing to her drinking habits'. Since then she had lived with Henry Turner, a carpenter, but though he claimed that when she was sober they got on well, they had recently parted, again because of her drinking. Turner had seen her on the Saturday before her death and had given her money to buy stock for sale, though 'when she had money she spent it in drink'.

Tabram had spent the last evening of her life with a fellow prostitute, Mary Ann Connolly, known as 'Pearly Poll', who told the inquest that they had been with two soldiers, a corporal and a private who had 'white bands round their caps'. They had drunk ale and rum for nearly two hours in a number of different pubs before parting just before midnight, when Tabram had gone off with the private. By the time the adjourned inquest resumed, attempts had been made to identify the men. Connolly had been to Wellington Barracks and had picked out two soldiers of the Coldstream Guards

> who were, to the best of her belief, the men she and Tabram
> were with… One of [those] picked out turned out not to be a
> corporal, but he had stripes on his arm … and he was proved
> beyond doubt to have been with his wife from 8 o'clock on the
> Monday night until 6 o'clock the following morning. The other
> man was also proved to have been in barracks at five minutes
> past ten on Bank Holiday night.

Detective Inspector Reid testified in addition that several witnesses had claimed to see Tabram with a corporal on the Sunday before her death, 'but when all the corporals and privates at the Tower and Wellington Barracks were paraded before them they failed to identify the man'.

The police had gone to great lengths to chase up the potential military connection, but when nothing came of it they had no further leads. It remains possible that Martha Tabram was killed by a soldier: the company she was keeping on the night of her death, along with the possibility that some of her wounds were made by a military weapon, leaves the question open. The inquest into her death was a relatively perfunctory affair, spread over only two days and meriting just a few paragraphs in the newspapers. But when the Nichols murder followed on so quickly, links were inevitably made between two such violent incidents in the same small area of London and within only a few weeks of each other. Once again the victim was a prostitute; once again the weapon was a sharp knife used with considerable brutality. The Nichols inquest, which opened on the day after the murder, Saturday 1 September, was much lengthier and more detailed. It is clear that the authorities realized they had a major investigation on their hands.

THE KILLER EMERGES

When PC Neil walked down Buck's Row on his regular beat in the early hours of 31 August, as he described to the coroner, the street was dark and deserted, lit only by a dim lamp at its end. The body of the murdered woman, lying on the pavement, was still quite warm, and he could see by the light from his lamp that there was blood oozing from her throat. He hailed two other policemen and sent them for the doctor and an ambulance, but though he noted that her clothes were disarranged, he did not find the wounds that had been inflicted on her abdomen. The coroner asked him whether he had heard any noise: 'No; I heard nothing. The farthest I had been that night was just through the Whitechapel Road and up Baker's Row. I was never far away from the spot... I saw a number of women in the main road going home. At that time any one could have got away.' He had knocked on the doors of the houses on the other side of the street but no one there had heard anything either.

Mary Ann Nichols was described as aged about 45, height 5ft 2in or 3in, complexion dark, hair dark brown (turning grey),

eyes brown, dressed in a 'brown ulster with seven large brass
buttons (figure of a female riding a horse and man at side
thereon), brown linsey frock, grey woollen petticoat ... brown
stays, black ribbed woollen stockings...'. The police report
(MEPO 3/140), signed by Inspector Spratling, was countersigned
by Superintendent Keating, who added a note in his own hand,
'It has since been ascertained that the dress bears the marks of
Lambeth Workhouse and deceased is supposed to have been an
inmate of that house.'

Dr Llewellyn's inquest testimony added further details of
what he had found when he examined her body:

Her hands and wrists were cold, but the body and lower
extremities were warm. I examined her chest and felt the
heart... I believe she had not been dead more than half an
hour... On the left side of the neck, about an inch below the jaw,
there was an incision about four inches long and running from
a point immediately below the ear. An inch below on the same
side, and commencing about an inch in front of it, was a circular
incision terminating at a point about three inches below the
right jaw. This incision completely severs all the tissues down to
the vertebrae. The large vessels of the neck on both sides were
severed. The incision is about eight inches long. These cuts
must have been caused with a long-bladed knife, moderately
sharp, and used with great violence. No blood at all was found
on the breast either of the body or clothes. There were no
injuries about the body till just about the lower part of the
abdomen. Two or three inches from the left side was a wound

running in a jagged manner. It was a very deep wound, and the tissues were cut through. There were several incisions running across the abdomen. On the right side there were also three or four similar cuts running downwards. All these had been caused by a knife, which had been used violently and been used downwards. The wounds were from left to right, and might have been done by a left-handed person. All the injuries had been done by the same instrument.

So another violent knife attack, and this time the killer had deliberately set out to disembowel his victim. In addition to the knife wounds, the doctor noted bruises on Nichols' face and neck, probably the result of pressure from fingers. Silently and ruthlessly, it seems, the murderer had throttled his victim until she was semi-conscious, before killing her with two great slashes across the throat and then moving down to her abdomen to slash that too.

Police enquiries revealed that Mary Ann Nichols had last been seen alive at 2.30 am

in a state of drunkenness at the corner of Osborn Street and Whitechapel Road, by Ellen Holland. She was then alone and going in the direction of Buck's Row … She told Ellen Holland that then she had no money to pay for her bed… Enquiry was made into her history which turns out to be as follows: the deceased through her intemperate habits separated from her husband about nine years ago and he allowed her 5s per week till 1882 when it came to his knowledge that she was leading an immoral life and he stopped the allowance. (HO 144/221/A49301C)

Nichols' father, Edward Walker, a retired smith, was the first witness at the inquest, and formally identified her body. He told the coroner, 'I was not on speaking terms with her. She had been living with me three or four years previously, but thought she could better herself, so I let her go.' In response to questions from the court Walker testified that 'at times she drank, and that was why we did not agree', but that to the best of his knowledge she was not guilty of improper behaviour or of being 'fast'. He also claimed that 'when she was confined her husband took on with the young woman who came to nurse her, and they parted, he living with the nurse, by whom he has another family'. When the coroner commented that 'she must have drunk heavily for you to turn her out of doors', his response was 'I never turned her out. She had no need to be like this while I had a home for her.' And his final words in evidence were that he could throw no light on why she might have been murdered: 'I don't think she had any enemies, she was too good for that.'

Another of her acquaintances told a different tale. Mary Ann Monk, a fellow inmate of Lambeth Workhouse, was quoted in the 1 September issue of the *Pall Mall Gazette* as saying that Nichols had left the workhouse to take a situation as servant at Ingleside, Wandsworth Common, and 'it afterwards became known that Nichols betrayed her trust as domestic servant by stealing £3 from her employer and absconding. From that time she had been wandering about. Monk met her, she said, about six weeks ago, when herself out of the workhouse, and drank with her.' Nichols was a flawed woman, therefore—thief, prostitute and down-and-out—but could still inspire fondness in her father and make friends among those in a similar situation.

Establishing the facts of the crimes would clearly be a challenge for the police. Chief Inspector Donald Swanson was the senior policeman appointed by Scotland Yard to enquire into the Whitechapel murders, reporting to Dr Robert Anderson, Assistant Commissioner (Crime) of the Met (see plate 11). His deputy was Inspector Frederick George Abberline, who had been in the police force for 25 years, the last 14 of them as Local Inspector in the Whitechapel CID (see plate 6). He therefore knew the area well. But investigative techniques available to the police at this time were limited. Fingerprint recognition was still in the future, as were other forensic aids. The police's best hope was either to catch a criminal in the act—and policemen on the beat were clearly far more common then, so this was not totally unlikely—or to receive information from witnesses or acquaintances of the perpetrator.

After Nichols' murder, suspicions had first fallen on criminal gangs operating in Whitechapel who set upon street women in the early hours of the morning, blackmailing them and inflicting violence if the women failed to pay up. But the police now deduced from the nature of Nichols' wounds—and Dr Llewellyn's belief that the killer knew something of anatomy—that a slaughterman might have been responsible for her death. They interviewed three men named Tomkins, Britton and Mumford, who were employed by night at a slaughterhouse, Messrs Harrison Barber & Co, in nearby Winthrop Street, but all could prove that they were not involved. Now too the name of John Pizer came up. Better known as 'Leather Apron', he was said by the women in the common lodging houses in Whitechapel to have blackmailed prostitutes and assaulted them if they did not comply with his requests for money. 'Leather Apron' rapidly gained currency as a name for the murderer, but Pizer himself could not at this stage be found.

By now the press floodgates had opened. All the London newspapers, and many others both national and international, were on the scent of the sensational story. The day after the murder, the *Star* of 1 September 1888 vented its outrage in thundering headlines: 'SPECIAL EDITION. THE WHITE-CHAPEL HORROR. THE THIRD CRIME OF A MAN WHO MUST BE A MANIAC.' The story was reeled out in over 1,300 words of lurid prose:

> The victim of the latest Whitechapel horror—the woman … was found yesterday morning in Buck's Row completely disembowelled and with her head nearly gashed from her body… There is a terribly significant similarity between this ghastly crime and the two mysterious murders of women which have occurred in the same district within the last three months. In each case the victim has been a woman of abandoned character, each crime has been committed in the dark hours of the morning, and more important still as pointing to one man, and that man a maniac, being the culprit, each murder has been

accompanied by hideous mutilation… Each of the ill-lighted thoroughfares to which the women were decoyed to be foully butchered are off turnings from Whitechapel Road, and all are within half a mile. The fact that these three tragedies have been committed within such a limited area, and are so strangely alike in their details, is forcing on all minds the conviction that they are the work of some cool, cunning man with a mania for murder. At present clues to the murder are entirely lacking…

There were in fact some potential leads. A man who kept a coffee stall on the corner of Whitechapel Road and Cambridge Road testified to the police that (as the *Star* went on to report):

at three o'clock yesterday morning a woman answering the description of the deceased came to his stall in company with a man five feet three or four inches high, dressed in a dark coat and black Derby hat, apparently about thirty-five years old. He had a black moustache and whiskers, and was fidgety and uneasy. He refused to have anything to eat, but paid for the woman's coffee. He grumbled and kept telling her to hurry, as he wished to get home.

However, the coffee stall keeper then became unsure whether it was the same woman. After viewing the remains, he felt that, if it was, she had (rather rapidly, it seems) grown thinner in the face.

The link made by the *Star* between the three murders was disingenuous: Smith's killing had not been 'accompanied by hideous mutilation', brutal though the attack was. But the newspapers were right to identify a pattern. The first three 'Whitechapel murders' had occurred, the last two of which could justifiably be considered as the acts of an emerging serial killer. The victims were prostitutes who lived and plied their trade in a small area within the slums of east London. Little is known about Smith, but both Tabram and Nichols were getting on for middle age, separated from their families and drunk on the nights they were killed; both were out late and both lived in common lodging houses, scraping a living mainly by selling their bodies and anything else they could.

The murderer too was beginning to emerge from the shadows: a man possessing some skill with a knife, and willing to take extreme risks to satisfy what must have been an overwhelming blood lust. The doctor's view that most of the 39 stabs on Martha Tabram's body were made while she was still alive implies a sadistic pleasure in inflicting pain. Yet even that was not enough for the killer: he wanted to mutilate the bodies of his victims, and to do so he had to kill them quickly so that they could not scream or fight back. It is clear that he worked very fast. When PC Neil walked through Buck's Row the street was quiet and peaceful; only half an hour later bloody murder had been done. The killer must have been gone only a few minutes. Is it possible that he was disturbed by the two men who saw Nichols' body just before PC Neil turned up again, and that he had planned further disembowelling? Or was his compulsion to 'rip' only just beginning to take hold?

CHAPTER TWO

A Maniac at Large

Mary Ann Nichols was buried on 7 September 1888 in the City of London cemetery. In the early hours of the next morning, the killer struck again. His victim was Annie Chapman, whose violently mutilated body was found in the back yard of 29 Hanbury Street, Spitalfields (see plates 4 and 5). The discovery was made just after 6 am on 8 September, by John Davis, a delivery man from Leadenhall Market who lived in the house with his wife and three sons. As he told the inquest, which opened on the Monday after the murder, 10 September, he had been woken at a quarter to six by the striking of the Spitalfields church clock, had had a cup of tea and gone down to the back yard:

> Directly I opened the door I saw a woman lying down in the left hand recess, between the stone steps [three of them, leading down from the passage between the front and back doors of the house to the slightly lower yard] and the fence. She was on her back, with her head towards the house and her legs towards the wood shed. The clothes were up to her groins. I did not go into the yard, but left the house by the front door, and called the attention of two men to the circumstances.

The two men ran off to find a policeman, while Davis went to Commercial Street police station to report what he had found. Another resident, Amelia Richardson, testified at the inquest that she had been wakeful during the night. She had also delivered a wake-up call just before 4 am to a fellow lodger called Thompson and had heard him leave via the front door. But she heard no other noise, though she claimed that she usually did hear people going through the passage to the back yard: 'People are coming in or going out all the night ... [but] I did not hear any one going through on Saturday morning.'

In common with most of the houses in the area, neither the front nor the back door of 29 Hanbury Street could be locked, and all those who knew the area must have been aware that it was easy to pass through from the street to the comparative privacy of the back yard. It seems that such occurrences were not uncommon. On this occasion, Mrs Richardson thought that the intruders must have walked quietly or she would have heard them. It was not until after 6 am, when she heard a lot of noise in the passage and sent her grandson down to investigate, that she found out about the murder.

Mrs Richardson may, however, have slept more heavily than she thought, because she appears to have failed to hear the arrival of her son John, who went to the house between 4.45 am and 4.50 am on that Saturday morning to check that the cellar was securely padlocked. They had suffered a burglary a few weeks previously and since then he had tended to look in on market mornings to check that all was well. As he told the court, he opened the yard door and sat down for a couple of minutes on the steps to cut a piece of leather off his boot, and could not have failed to notice the deceased if she had been lying there. And another witness, Elizabeth Long, had seen a woman she was sure was the victim talking to a man in Hanbury Street at about 5.30 am:

> I have seen the deceased in the mortuary, and I am sure the woman that I saw was the deceased. I did not see the man's face, but I noticed that he was dark. He was wearing a brown low-crowned felt hat. I think he had on a dark coat, though I am not certain. By the look of him he seemed to me a man over forty years of age. He appeared to me to be a little taller than the deceased… He looked like a foreigner … like what I should call shabby-genteel… They were talking pretty loudly. I over-heard him say to her 'Will you?' and she replied 'Yes.'

If Mrs Long was right, the murder had taken place in the 40 or so minutes between this sighting at 5.30 am and 6.10 am when John Davis found the body. Once again the killer was showing enormously bold behaviour—and even more so in this case. As it emerged at the inquest, he had taken time to eviscerate the body and remove some of the organs. The risks were extraordinary: it was getting light, people were up and about, moving around the area on their way to work and market, and the flimsy houses were full of those who might have challenged him. Yet he managed to lure Chapman into the yard, kill her and viciously mutilate her body without being seen or heard. And he must have walked away through increasingly light and bustling streets, possibly splattered with blood and carrying a bag containing some of his victim's innards.

The killer inflicted terrible injuries on Chapman's body. As the police report detailed:

> the throat was severed deeply, incision jagged. Removed from but attached to body and placed above right shoulder were a flap of the wall of belly, the whole of the small intestines and attachments. Two other portions of wall of belly and [genitals] were placed above left shoulder in a large quantity of blood… The following parts were missing: part of belly wall including navel; the womb, the upper part of vagina and greater part of bladder. The doctor gives it as his opinion that the murderer was possessed of anatomical knowledge from the manner of removal of viscera, and that the knife used was not an ordinary knife, but such as a small amputating knife, or a well ground slaughterman's knife, narrow and thin, sharp and blade of six to eight inches in length. (HO 144/221/A49301C)

The evidence given at the inquest by George Baxter Phillips, divisional surgeon of police, corroborated this report, but added that there was evidence that the victim had been partially strangled: 'The face was swollen and turned on the right side, and the tongue protruded between the front teeth, but not beyond the lips; it was much swollen.' He also testified that it must have taken the murderer at least a quarter of an hour to carry out all the mutilations, and added the detail that the legs were drawn up, with the feet resting on the ground and the knees turned outwards—her limbs presumably arranged in this fashion by the killer in order to allow himself easy access to her abdomen. Dr Phillips was deeply reluctant to give full details of what had been done to Chapman's body in open court because he felt that it would be too disgusting for general distribution. He tried to persuade the coroner that his evidence about the fatal wounds was enough for the court's purposes, but the coroner and the jury were having none of it.

Apart from Elizabeth Long, the last known people to see Chapman alive were the deputy and the nightwatchman of the common lodging house where she had lived for the previous four months. Timothy Donovan, the deputy, identified her body and told the police that at 2 am Chapman was under the influence of drink and had left the lodging house to get money to pay for her bed: 'She had had enough [to drink]; of that I am certain... She was very sociable in the kitchen. I said to her, "You can find money for your beer, and you can't find money for your bed."' She asked him not to let her bed to anyone else, and left the house, going through a court called Paternoster Street, into Brushfield Street and then towards Spitalfields church.

Another resident of the lodging house, Amelia Palmer, had known Chapman well for five years, and believed her to be the widow of Frederick Chapman, a Windsor veterinary surgeon— actually a coachman—who had died about 18 months previously. Chapman had left her two children and her husband around four years before, and he had given her an allowance of 10s a week. It was only when this allowance ceased that she heard about her husband's death, and since then it seemed that she had led an even more hand-to-mouth existence. Mrs Palmer told the coroner that Chapman had recently been involved in at least one brawl with another woman which had left her with bruises on her face and chest, and that she had given Chapman 2d for a cup of tea one day when she had seen her looking pale and ill. 'She used to do crochet work, make antimacassars and sell flowers. She was out late at night at times. On Fridays she used to go to Stratford to sell anything she had.' But on the last Friday of her life she had told Mrs Palmer:

> 'I feel too ill to do anything... It is of no use my going away. I shall have to go somewhere to get some money to pay my lodgings.' She said no more, and that was the last time that I saw her... Since the death of her husband she has seemed to give way altogether.

The similarities between this murder and that of Mary Ann Nichols were obvious, and once again Inspector Abberline was assigned to the case. It seemed that a breakthrough had been made when, two days after Chapman's murder, John Pizer— 'Leather Apron'—was found and arrested by Detective Sergeant William Thicke. Pizer had been lying low at 22 Mulberry Street, the home of his stepmother and his brother, and

> he turned very pale when he recognized the officer, whom he had encountered on a previous occasion and he exclaimed,

'Mother, he has got me,' or words to that effect … He was led to Leman Street police station unperceived until close to the door of the station, when the cry was raised, 'Leather Apron!' and, as usual, there was a hostile demonstration. (*Echo*, 11 September 1888)

When he appeared before the coroner, Pizer admitted to being the man nicknamed 'Leather Apron'. But he testified that he had been at 22 Mulberry Street from 6 September until he was arrested there by Sergeant Thicke on the following Monday. He had, on his brother's advice, remained indoors the whole time because 'I was the object of a false suspicion… I wish to vindicate my character to the world at large.' He was able to prove that at the time of the Nichols murder he was in another part of London altogether, and even before his appearance at the inquest, the police had checked his alibis and released him. By an odd coincidence, John Richardson owned a leather apron which his mother had brought up from the cellar of 29 Hanbury Street on 6 September to wash it clear of mildew. She left it by the water pump in the back yard and it was still lying there when Annie Chapman was murdered. But from now on suspicion of 'Leather Apron' more or less ceased.

In the absence of an arrest, press activity grew more frenzied and criticism of the police more pointed. The newspapers demanded to know why the police had not found bloodstains in the yard of 25 Hanbury Street, two houses away from the murder scene, which had been pointed out by a little girl who lived there. As *The Times* for 12 September reported:

> a bloody trail was found distinctly marked for a distance of
> five or six feet in the direction of the back door of the house.
> Further investigation left no doubt that the trail was that of
> the murderer, who, it was evident, after finishing his work had
> passed through or over the dividing fence between nos 29 and
> 27, and thence into the garden of no 25. On the wall of the last
> house there was found a curious mark, between a smear and a
> sprinkle, which had probably been made by the murderer, who,
> alarmed by the blood-soaked state of his coat, took off that
> garment and knocked it against the wall.

The day before, under screaming headlines, the *Echo* had described the excitable scenes in the murder streets:

> From morning till night crowds of people were yesterday
> lounging about the police office in Commercial Street, in
> Hanbury Street, and in Buck's Row. The crowd was swelled
> as the day progressed by the innumerable loungers to whom
> Monday is a holiday, and by inquisitive scores from more civil-
> ized portions of the Metropolis—two well-known peers being
> amongst this number... Slatternly women, hulking, ruffianly
> men, crowds of better-dressed observers flocked to the scene.
> Hanbury Street was, however, the more popular resort of the
> town. In front of the fatal house a great crowd stood all day,
> extending a considerable way up and down the street.

There was further excitement when a suspect with blood on his
clothes and wounds on his hands was arrested in Gravesend;

but he proved to be a man of unsound mind with no connection at all to the murders. There was, however, another more credible suspect—a butcher called Joseph Isenschmid (see plate 7)—who was brought to the authorities' attention by two doctors and who had been seen on the morning of the Chapman murder with blood on his hands. His wife told the police that she had not seen him for two months though he had visited the house in her absence to collect clothing, and 'she further stated that he was in the habit of carrying large butcher's knives about with him' (MEPO 3/140). It emerged that he had meanwhile been detained in an infirmary and certified as a dangerous lunatic.

However, when Isenschmid was apprehended Sergeant Thicke examined his clothes and found no blood on them. It seems that he got his living through buying offcuts of meat in the market, preparing them and then selling them to restaurants and coffee houses in the West End. He could therefore show adequate reason for being up early, for carrying knives and for having bloody hands. Isenschmid too was eliminated from enquiries and was later confined in a mental hospital.

Despite the growing criticism of the police, surviving records show that their investigations were thorough. They had found the man who was Annie Chapman's regular consort, and were satisfied that he was not a suspect. A torn envelope with two pills in it had been found by Chapman's body, and the police had quickly discovered that this could be associated with the 1st Battalion of the Sussex Regiment quartered at Farnborough.

Although the envelope offered few clues, Inspector Abberline immediately sent Inspector Chandler to the depot to check up on it. Captain Young, Acting Adjutant, identified it as bearing the official stamp of the regiment; he also told the police that the majority of the men used this paper, which they purchased at the canteen. But enquiries yielded nothing more, and it turned out that a witness had seen Annie Chapman pick up a piece of paper at her lodging house to wrap pills she was taking. The envelope was yet another red herring.

Chapman's inquest was heard over five days, finishing on 26 September, and the proceedings were fully reported in the press. Public fascination with the murders was growing, and this fascination was soon to show its darker side. On 25 September a letter addressed to Sir Charles Warren, Commissioner of Police, and bearing the heading 'on her majesterys service', arrived at Scotland Yard in an unstamped envelope. The writer said he was a 'horse slauterer' and that he had claimed the victim he had been aiming for, Annie Chapman. Beginning with a show of penitence and confession—'I do wish to give myself up I am in misery with nightmare I am the man who committed all these murders in the last six months...'—the letter ended with the threat, 'keep the Boro road clear or I might take a trip up there...' Two black coffin shapes obscured the places where the sender had apparently written his name, and his address was similarly heavily blacked out. There was also a drawing of a knife which he said was the one he had used to commit the crimes:

'it is a small handle with a large long blade sharpe both sides'.

The police took little notice. Everything in the letter was public knowledge from the inquest reports that had appeared in the newspapers, and they were used to hoax mail in high profile cases. But a couple of days later, a second missive, dated 25 September but postmarked 27 September, was sent to the Central News Agency. It was to create the monster whose name is legendary to this day. This famous letter was the first to be signed 'Jack the Ripper'. Written in red ink, in what appears to be quite a well-schooled hand, it was addressed to 'Dear Boss':

> I keep on hearing the police have caught me but they wont fix me just yet. I have laughed when they look so clever and talk about being on the right track. That joke about Leather Apron gave me real fits. I am down on whores and I shant quit ripping them till I do get buckled. Grand work the last one was I gave the lady no time to squeal. How can they catch me now. I love my work and want to start again. You will soon hear of me with my funny little games. I saved some of the proper <u>red</u> stuff in a ginger beer bottle over the last job to write with but it went thick like glue and I cant use it. Red ink is fit enough I hope <u>ha ha</u>. The next job I do I shall clip the ladys ears off and send to the police officers just for jolly wouldnt you. Keep this letter back till I do a bit more work then give it out straight. My knifes so nice and sharp I want to get to work right away if I get a chance. Good luck. Yours truly Jack the Ripper Dont mind me giving the trade name.

At right angles below the signature, and now very faded, is a postscript: 'wasnt good enough to post this before I got all the red ink off my hands curse it. No luck yet. They say Im a doctor now <u>ha ha</u>' (see plate 8).

Two days later the Central News Agency forwarded it to Scotland Yard with a covering note saying that they had treated it as a joke. Whether or not the police initially took it seriously is not known. But the phenomenon was to become one of the defining features of the case, as letters from people claiming to be the murderer flooded police headquarters (MEPO 3/142 and 3/3153). And that very night the murderer was to strike again—not once but twice.

THWARTED BLOOD LUST

At 1 am in the early morning of 30 September Louis Diemshutz, the secretary of a socialist club at 40 Berner Street, was coming home, driving his pony and wagon. As he entered the club yard the pony shied at something lying on the ground. It was very dark, but when Diemshutz got down to investigate he found the body of a woman. He raised the alarm and it was only a few minutes before policemen and doctors arrived. The woman had only just been killed; her body was warm and blood was flowing copiously from her neck.

The club was still open and full of members coming and going, talking and singing. The street outside was also still bustling despite the late hour. Some of the people there claimed to have seen the woman shortly before her death: the greengrocer Matthew Packer, who had shut his shop only just before the murder, thought he may have sold grapes to a man who was with her; a James Brown had gone out at 12.45 am to buy his supper at a nearby chandler's and believed he had caught sight of her in the street; and a policeman, PC Smith, had seen her 10 minutes earlier talking to a man dressed in dark clothes who was carrying a parcel about 18 inches long wrapped in newspaper. It had been raining around midnight but the rain had stopped by the time the body was found, and the woman's clothes were dry. Everything therefore pointed to a murder committed suddenly and hastily between 12.45 and 1 am.

As police enquiries subsequently established, there had even been a sighting of a woman and a man struggling outside the yard gate of 40 Berner Street. According to Chief Inspector Donald Swanson's report of events, Israel Schwartz had been walking along the street and had just reached the gateway to the yard when he saw 'a man stop and speak to a woman, who was standing in the gateway. The man tried to pull the woman into the street, but he turned her round and threw her down on the footway and the woman screamed three times but not very loudly' (HO 144/221/A49301C). There was another man on the scene, standing nearby lighting his pipe, and Schwartz heard the attacker shouting the word 'Lipski', though he was not sure at whom the shout had been aimed or whether the two men knew each other. He then left. Schwartz later identified the body in the mortuary as that of the woman he had seen being man-handled, and provided a description of her assailant: 'age about thirty, height 5ft 5in, complexion fair, hair dark, small brown moustache, full face, broad shouldered, dress dark jacket and trousers, black cap with peak, had nothing in his hands'.

Inspector Abberline believed that the shout of 'Lipski' was aimed at Schwartz:

> since a Jew named Lipski was hanged for the murder of a Jewess in 1887 the name has very frequently been used by persons as a mere ejaculation by way of endeavouring to insult the Jew to whom it has been addressed, and as Schwartz has a strong Jewish appearance I am of opinion it was addressed to him as he stopped to look at the man he saw apparently ill using the deceased woman. (MEPO 3/140)

So the shout of 'Lipski' may well have been a deadly insult cal-culated to drive a possible witness away from the place where the killer was about to commit another murder.

The victim was Elizabeth Stride, a Swede who had lived in England for several decades and spoke perfect English (see plate 10). She was identified by fellow residents of a nearby common lodging house, where she had lived on and off for six years or more and was known as 'Long Liz' because of her height. She had also lived for three years with a man named Michael Kidney, but had sometimes left him for short periods and had done so just two days before she was killed. Her acquaintances testified that

she was a sober woman, and had earned 6d on that Saturday by
cleaning two rooms in the lodging house before leaving the house
in the early evening. By the time of her death she had bought or
been given a flower which was pinned to her breast, and she had
been seen before midnight consorting happily with a man.

Another lone woman had been viciously and speedily murdered. If the killer was the man who had carried out the awful
mutilations on the bodies of his previous two victims, it seems
all too likely that he had intended to do the same—but this time
he had been disturbed. Perhaps he had heard Louis Diemshutz
driving up to the gate of the yard and slipped out before he
could be noticed; perhaps the loud singing in the club made him
wary of spending any more time at the scene. But his blood lust
was rampant. Whatever his reason for abandoning his first victim, he hastened off to find another woman to kill and violate.

CLUES AND RED HERRINGS

It did not take long. At 1.30 am, as PC Edward Watkins of the
City Police later testified, he walked through Mitre Square on
his regular beat, and found that all was quiet. Just 15 minutes
later, at 1.45, he came across the horribly mutilated body of a
woman lying in a pool of blood in a dark corner of the square
behind an unoccupied house. As he told a reporter from the
Star who accompanied him to the scene:

it didn't take me a moment to see that the Whitechapel murderer had been our way. Her head lay here on this coal-hole …
and her clothes were thrown up breast-high. But the first thing
I noticed was that she was ripped up like a pig in the market.
There was the big gash up the stomach, the entrails torn out
and flung in a heap about her neck; some of them appeared to
be lying in the ugly cut at the throat, and the face—well, there
was no face. Anyone who knew the woman alive would never
recognize her by her face. I have been in the force a long while,
but I never saw such a sight. (*Star*, 1 October 1888)

It later emerged that one of the victim's kidneys and her womb
had been removed and taken away, and part of her right ear had
been cut off.

She was identified as Catherine Eddowes, also known as
Mary Kelly, who had spent several hours of the evening before
her death in the cells at Bishopsgate police station after being
found lying in a drunken stupor in Aldgate (see plate 9). The
gaoler had checked up on her several times during the evening,
and eventually found her awake and singing to herself at about
12.30. Half an hour later he released her and saw her turn left
towards Houndsditch on her way home, a route that would have
taken her close to Mitre Square. Half an hour after that, Joseph
Lawende and two other men, who had spent the evening in a
nearby club and were just leaving to go home, saw her with a
man in a corner of the square.

Mitre Square is about three-quarters of a mile—a 10-minute

walk—away from Berner Street, just within the borders of the City of London (which brought this murder within the jurisdiction of a different police authority, the City of London Police, with consequently different personnel and unfortunately few surviving records). The description of the man seen in Mitre Square differed in several respects from that of the man seen earlier in Berner Street; but this time there was a further clue. Just before 3 am, a police officer walking up Goulston Street, a few streets away from Mitre Square, found in a doorway a piece of bloodied cloth which proved to have been cut from the apron worn by Catherine Eddowes. The murderer had, it seems, retraced his steps towards Whitechapel, discarding the piece of apron on the way. It seems that Whitechapel was his main stamping ground, his excursion into the City probably an unplanned reaction to having been disturbed earlier.

Again, the Ripper had worked with phenomenal speed: accosting Eddowes, slashing her throat, cutting her up and walking away with parts of her body. This murder, like that of Elizabeth Stride less than an hour before, had taken 15 minutes at most. And this time his frenzied attack appears to have been even more violent than those he had inflicted on Nichols and Chapman. Not only were some of Eddowes' viscera taken, as had happened with Chapman, but her face was considerably cut too. Was his blood lust heightened by his failure to complete his work on Stride's body?

There are several theories about the apron. Had the killer

1 Whitechapel Street in the late Victorian period: a bustling community into which the murderer could all too easily slip unnoticed after his crimes.

2 *Above*: PC Neil finding Mary Ann Nichols' body in Bucks Row; the drawing accurately reflects his description of the scene as given at the inquest.

3 *Right*: The first page of Inspector John Spratling's report on the Nichols murder after he had discovered the mutilations on her body at the mortuary. (MEPO 3/140)

31st August 1888

P.C. 97 J. Neil, reports at 3.45. a.
31st inst. he found the dead body of a
woman lying on her back with her clo—
a little above her knees, with her thr—
cut from ear to ear on a yard crossi—
at Bucks Row, Whitechapel, P.C.
obtained the assistance of P.C. 55. H.
Smizen and 96 H. Thain, the latter call
Dr Llewellyn, No 152. Whitechapel Ro—
he arrived quickly and pronounced
life to be extinct, apparently but
few minutes, he directed her remov—
to the Mortuary, stating he would m—
a further examination there, whi—
was done on the Ambulance.

Upon my arrival there and
taking a description I found that
she had been disembowelled, and at
once sent to inform the Dr of it, h—
arrived quickly and on further exam—
ination stated that her throat had
been cut from left to right, two dist—
cuts being on left side, the windp—
gullet and spinal cord being cut
through, a bruise apparently of a th—
being on right lower jaw, also one o—
left cheek, the abdomen had been
open from centre of bottom of ribs o—
right side, under pelvis to left of the

4 *Above*: The yard at the back of 29 Hanbury Street where Annie Chapman's body was discovered lying in the space between the fence and the steps.

5 *Left*: Annie Chapman in the mortuary. (MEPO 3/3155)

when he left home he had in his possession two large knives that he used in his business. He is now confined in the Bow Infirmary Asylum Fairfield Road. Bow. and Dr. Mickle has been seen with a View to arrange for Mrs. Fiddymont and other witnesses to see him. but the doctors thinks this cannot be done at present with safety to his patient.

As time is of the greatest importance in this case. not only with regard to the question of identity, but also for the purpose of allaying the strong public feeling that exists I would respectfully suggest that either the Chief Surgeon, or one of the Divl. Surgeons may be requested to see Dr. Mickle the resident medical Officer to make if possible some arrangements for the witnesses &c to see Isenschmid.

Ch. Insp. Swanson.
Rec. 5 A.C. 6 JB.
(15)

F. G. Abberline Insp.
Chisholme Sup.

6 *Above*: Inspector Frederick Abberline was the police officer most familiar with the East End and most involved with the on-the-ground Ripper investigation.

7 *Left*: The final page of Inspector Abberline's report on the Nichols and Chapman murders, dated 19 September 1888, with regard to the suspect Isenschmid. (MEPO 3/140)

25. Sept. 1888.

Dear Boss

I keep on hearing the police have caught me. but they wont fix me just yet. I have laughed when they look so clever and talk about being on the right track. That joke about Leather Apron gave me real fits. I am down on whores and I shant quit ripping them till I do get buckled. Grand work the last job was. I gave the lady no time to squeal. How can they catch me now. I love my work and want to start again. you will soon hear of me with my funny little games. I saved some of the proper red stuff in a ginger beer bottle over the last job to write with but it went thick like glue and I cant use it. Red ink is fit enough I hope ha. ha. The next job I do I shall clip the ladys ears off and send to the

police officers just for jolly wouldnt you. Keep this letter back till I do a bit more work then give it out straight. My Knife's so nice and sharp I want to get to work right away if I get a chance. Good luck.

yours truly

Jack the Ripper

Dont mind me giving the trade name

wasnt good enough to post this before I got all the red ink off my hands curse it. No luck yet. They say I am a doctor now. ha ha

8 *Above*: The famous 'Dear Boss' letter, the first to be signed 'Jack the Ripper' and the first of scores of hoax letters to the police carrying that signature. (MEPO 3/142)

9 *Right*: Catherine Eddowes, killed in Mitre Square on the night of the 'double event', 30 September 1888.

10 *Opposite*: Mortuary photograph of Elizabeth Stride, the third of the 'canonical five' Ripper victims. (MEPO 3/3156)

METROPOLITAN POLICE.

CRIMINAL INVESTIGATION DEPARTMENT,
SCOTLAND YARD,

6th day of November 1888

HOME OFFICE
6 NOV. 88
WH OF DEPT

CENTRAL OFFICER'S
SPECIAL REPORT.

SUBJECT *Jack knows*
Met: Police respecting the
murders in Mitre Square &
thief on wall.

REFERENCE TO PAPERS.

I beg to report that the facts concerning the murder in Mitre Square which came to the Knowledge of the Metropolitan Police are as follows:—

1.45 a.m. 30th Sept. Police Constable Watkins of the City Police discovered in Mitre Square the body of a woman, with her face mutilated almost beyond identity, portion of the nose being cut off, the lobe of the right ear nearly severed, the face cut; the throat cut, and disembowelled. The P.C. called to his assistance Mr Morris, a night watchman and pensioner from Metrop: police, from premises looking on the Square. and surgical aid was subsequently called in, short details of which will be given further on in this report.

11 *Above*: Chief Inspector Donald Swanson was the senior Scotland Yard detective in overall charge of the Ripper enquiries.

12 *Left*: The first page of Swanson's report for the Metropolitan Police on the Eddowes murder, which fell within the jurisdiction of the City of London Police. (HO 144/221/A49301C) perhaps carved a piece off to wipe away the blood on his hands and knife, or to serve as a makeshift bag for his trophies while making a quick getaway? Could he have heard PC Watkins returning to the square, and been forced to improvise hastily? In the comparative shelter of Goulston Street, a few minutes later, did he transfer his bloody cargo into a more suitable container and discard the piece of apron?

And did he then, on the spur of the moment, decide to leave a red herring for the police? For chalked on the wall in the entryway where the apron was found was one of the most enigmatic 'documents' of the Ripper case. At shoulder height just inside the archway were the following words:

> The Juwes are
> The men that
> Will not
> Be Blamed
> For nothing

The killer may not have written those words. But, intriguingly, there was a strong Jewish aspect to this 'double event' on 30 September. Many of the members of the socialist club where Stride had been killed were Jews. It was a strikingly Jewish man who had witnessed the manhandling in Berner Street outside the club. The men who had walked through Mitre Square just before the murder and had seen Eddowes were Jewish. And of course Whitechapel had a large and vibrant Jewish community. It is at least possible that the murderer decided to point the finger at a member of that community as the perpetrator of his crimes.

The surviving reports of the police investigation (see plate 12) reveal painstaking attempts to follow every lead and chase down every possible clue. Yet what followed in Goulston Street that morning must be the most inept piece of police decision-making in the whole case—and it was the decision of the top man, Metropolitan Police Commissioner Sir Charles Warren (see plates 19 and 20). Inspector McWilliam of the City police force had ordered the chalked inscription to be photographed, a procedure that was not standard at the time and would have taken at least an hour to carry out. But both Sir Charles and Superintendent Arnold of the Met were worried that the streets were about to become thronged with people, including many Jews, and that the inscription might cause a riot. Although he did at least ensure that a copy was made, Sir Charles therefore ordered it to be sponged away. He was a military man by profession, not a policeman, which may be why he appears to have been cavalier with potentially valuable evidence. And although police records of the time studiously avoid apportioning blame, the City Police Commissioner, Sir Henry Smith, later pointed the finger firmly at Sir Charles, calling his decision to expunge the writing 'an unpardonable blunder'.

Sir Charles' good intentions misfired almost immediately. The inscription and a great deal of debate about its meaning were splashed all over the newspapers, and his misguided action attracted further scorn when another communication from 'Jack the Ripper' arrived at the Central News Agency on the Monday after the two murders. Any possibility of comparing the handwriting of the Goulston Street inscription with this new missive and the earlier 'Dear Boss' letter was now impossible. And the contents of this new note were intriguing, because they referred both to the earlier letter, which had not yet been made public, and to the 'double event' of the previous night. What's more, both letters seemed at first reading to show privileged access to the full details of the crimes.

This second Ripper note, accessible today in facsimile though the original is now missing from the National Archives, became known as the 'saucy Jacky' postcard (see plate 13). Postmarked 1 October, it was heavily smeared with blood in which the fingerprint of its writer could be seen. It read:

> I was not codding dear old Boss when I gave you the tip, you'll hear about saucy Jackys work tomorrow double event this time number one squealed a bit couldn't finish straight off had not time to get ears for police thanks for keeping last letter back till I got to work again. Jack the Ripper.

The writing on this postcard bore some resemblance to that of the 'Dear Boss' letter, though it was scrawled more untidily. But its reference to the earlier letter and to its promise to cut off the ears of the next victim initially convinced the police that the same person had written both communications, and that that person might be the killer. At the very least, the writer clearly had close access to the facts, though the detailed press coverage of the crimes would have allowed everyone who read newspapers to know exactly what had been done to the victims. At any event, the police believed that the two letters were important enough to be made public, in the hope that someone might come forward and identify the handwriting. So they were reproduced on posters displayed at many London police stations from 3 October, and were also published in the press (see also plate 16).

There had now been six Whitechapel murders in six months, if Emma Smith is included—and five within only two months. All of those five were clearly the work of one or more maniacal knifemen disposed to hate prostitutes. The East End of London was in uproar. As the *Star* of 1 October proclaimed:

> The terror of Whitechapel has walked again, and this time has marked down two victims, one hacked and disfigured beyond discovery, the other with her throat cut and torn. Again he has got away clear; and again the police, with wonderful frankness, confess that they have not a clue. They are waiting for a seventh and an eighth murder, just as they waited for a fifth, to help them to it. Meanwhile, Whitechapel is half mad with fear. The people are afraid even to talk with a stranger … the spirit of terror has got fairly abroad, and no one knows what steps a practically defenceless community may take to protect itself or avenge itself.

And that enemy now had a horror-filled name—Jack the Ripper.

CHAPTER THREE

—

The Final Act?

══

'No one could say there were not enough police in the East End today. The blue helmets were thick as bees in a clover field, and there was a detective to about every three uniformed men on duty as well.' This was how the *Star* reported the scenes in Whitechapel later on the Sunday of the 'double event' murders of Elizabeth Stride and Catherine Eddowes:

> By eleven o'clock it seemed as if the entire population of the East End was out of doors. Streams of all sorts and conditions of men poured incessantly in the direction of Berner Street and of Mitre Square. Cordons of police blocked the three entrances to the latter, but the sensation-seeking crowds seemed to gather some satisfaction from mere proximity to the spot where the curtain had last been raised on the terrible series of tragedies.

Superintendent Foster of the City Police, who was in charge of the investigation of the crime scene in Mitre Square, had to fight his way through the mob, particularly when he was seen with a man in a tweed suit as he came out of Berner Street. 'There they go. The super's got him. I told you he was a toff,' was the shout that went up, and the two men struggled to throw off what the *Star* described as their 'unwanted retinue'. The panic was at fever pitch, both on the streets and in the press, as the story was reported all over the country and the western world. On 1 October the news of the two new murders had already hit the American and Canadian papers, which carried full accounts under headlines such as those in the *Manitoba Daily Free Press*: 'Two women fall victims to the mad doctor's monomaniacal researches'.

On that same day too, 1 October, the first Jack the Ripper letters were published, not just nationally but internationally: the wording of the 'Dear Boss' letter appeared in the *Newark Daily Advocate* of Ohio, for example. At home, the *Star* made comparatively little of it, treating it as a hoax and burying the piece about it quite a long way down in its extensive coverage of the crimes. Other newspapers gave the correspondence more prominence: on 4 October the *Daily Telegraph* printed facsimiles of part of the 'Dear Boss' letter and of the 'saucy Jacky' postcard. Such coverage, along with the ubiquitous police posters in London showing the letter and postcard, reinforced the view that they were significant, even if no one quite believed they were from the pen of the killer.

The atrocities carried out on Catherine Eddowes' body intensified the belief that the murderer was a man with knowledge of anatomy. This fuelled the rumour rapidly spreading round the East End, that he must be a man of some education, possibly a doctor and therefore a 'toff'. The failure of the police to get anywhere with catching him was arousing growing fear and anger, made worse by the refusal of the Home Secretary, Henry Matthews, to offer a reward. A thick file of documents held by the National Archives (HO 144/220/A49301B) records the debate about the wisdom of rewards in cases such as this. The police had discontinued such rewards several years previously because they had been shown to be both ineffective and counter-productive. Yet the newspapers were baying for a reward, and the MP for Whitechapel, Samuel Montagu, himself offered £100 to anyone whose information led to the discovery and conviction of the murderer. The East End Vigilance Committee, which had been set up in response to the crimes under the chairmanship of local builder George Akin Lusk, sent a petition to the queen, asking her to direct Matthews to offer a reward. It was to no avail. As the file records, the petition was forwarded to the Home Office from Balmoral, with the message 'We have of course sent no reply from here.'

The police were constantly urged to use bloodhounds to follow the murderer's trail. Sir Charles Warren tested the idea by having himself pursued across Hyde Park as a personal experiment in October 1888, and then put in a requisition for £50 to be allocated to hiring such dogs, a sum which included £15 to buy a puppy which would be trained with an older dog. Internal Home Office memos (HO 144/221/A49301E), however, record a degree of scepticism about this measure:

bloodhounds should be kept constantly practised in the streets
if they are to be any use in towns… Just now public opinion
probably would condone any measure however extreme to
discover the murderer, but if the use of bloodhounds is to be
authorized I think it should be strictly limited to the present
emergency; an extraordinary proceeding for an extraordinary
crime—and every precaution should be observed in their use.
If an accident happened from the dogs attacking an innocent
person there would be a great outcry.

Press coverage of the investigation during October included
reports that suspicious-looking men had been arrested, some of
them suspected of being American or otherwise foreign. One
Austrian seaman was claimed to be the killer on the basis of his
signature, which apparently resembled that on the 'Dear Boss'
letter. It took little to arouse suspicion, as the civil servant
Arthur Munby (see pp. 5–6) found—merely being a lone man in
London or elsewhere was enough to evoke curiosity and speculation, and any sort of odd or eccentric behaviour was likely to
result in a report to the police, particularly if the suspected person was a doctor. One anonymous correspondent became very
agitated about the likeness he perceived between a cartoon doctor in a magazine called *Scraps*, who was portrayed as behaving
as a guilty man might, and a real doctor who had recently
moved into 51 Abingdon Road, Kensington. This likeness could
not be accidental, the correspondent claimed; the maker of the
drawing must know something and be using this medium to

alert the authorities. Chief Inspector Donald Swanson was suitably underwhelmed, and rejected it as 'the product of an excited imagination' (HO 144/220/A49301A).

The police were 'inundated with suggestions and names of suspects', as Sir Charles Warren wrote to his counterpart in the City Police, Sir James Fraser, when the two forces began to collaborate after the Eddowes murder. Later in October, Dr Robert Anderson summed up police frustration:

> That a crime of this kind should have been committed without any clue being supplied by the criminal is unusual, but that five successive murders should have been committed without our having the slightest clue of any kind is extraordinary, if not unique, in the annals of crime. The result has been to necessitate our giving attention to innumerable suggestions, such as would in any ordinary case be dismissed unnoticed, and no hint of any kind, which was not obviously absurd, has been neglected. Moreover, the activity of the police has been to a considerable extent wasted through the exigencies of sensational journalism, and the action of unprincipled persons who, from various motives, have endeavoured to mislead us. But on the other hand the public generally and especially the inhabitants of the East End have shown a marked desire to assist in every way, even at some sacrifice to themselves. (HO 144/221/A49301C)

Whitechapel was feeling the strain. Not only was there fear on the streets but trade was being driven away from the area. In late October around 160 Whitechapel tradesmen and women sent a petition to the Home Secretary, asking for a stronger police presence: 'The universal feeling prevalent in our midst is that the government no longer ensure the security of life and property in east London and that in consequence respectable people fear to go out shopping, thus depriving us of our means of livelihood' (MEPO 3/141). The petition worked: more police were deployed from other parts of London and every effort was made to reassure the populace of the East End that their safety was a priority.

The growing tide of hoax letters, with their taunting messages and promises of more murders to come, encroached increasingly on police time. Often, as with one letter sent to the *Star* on 1 October 1888, they were specific as to the number and timing of murders: 'I have done 6 I am going to do 14 more then go back to America the next time I shall do 3 in one night...' With a few exceptions, these letters were signed 'Jack the Ripper'. The pseudonym had well and truly caught the public imagination, and was now the name by which the murderer was widely known. A legend had been born.

It is clear from internal police and Home Office documents that the authorities regarded these letters—which continued for the rest of 1888 and through 1889 and beyond—as mischievous and time-consuming nuisances. But they nevertheless had to examine them all in case one actually might be from the killer. It was also important to try to identify the writers, both to eliminate them from enquiries and to ensure that they could be publicly vilified and punished as wasters of precious police time. This is arguably why the police chose to publicise the original 'Boss' correspondence so widely. As a tactic, though, it backfired. Along with the press reports, the letters simply provided further material for those misguided individuals who decided to masquerade in print as Jack the Ripper.

Most of the letters drew obvious inspiration from the original two, as is shown in the repetition of 'boss' and 'ha ha', the threat to cut off parts of the victim's body, the use of red ink, the language and tone. Some of them were grammatical and well spelled, others almost illiterate; some of the writing was even and legible, while in other cases it was a scrawl. Some contained drawings, of knives, bones, coffins or fanciful portraits of the Ripper himself, and a particularly vicious one sent to Sir Charles Warren included a childish drawing of Sir Charles with a balloon shape representing his liver coming out of his abdomen. The letter promised that:

> my next job will be to polish you off and as I am a member of the force I can soon settle accounts with you. I will tear your liver out before you are dead and show it to you and I will have your kidneys out also and fill them with pepper and salt and send them to Lord Salisbury as it is just the sort of thing that will suit that old Jew and I will cut of your toes slice of your behind and make macaroni soup of them and I will hide your body in the houses of parliament so you grey headed old pig say your prayers before I am ready. I cannot say any more at present boss yours truly Jack the Ripper.

This letter also betrays an oddity notable in some of the correspondence—apologies offered by the writer. In this case they
concerned the fact that he was currently in bed with a sore
throat but that as soon as it was better he would set to work
again. Others said sorry for the quality of the paper, some written in black apologised for not writing in red and some of those
posted without a stamp bemoaned the fact that the writer could
not afford one. Several of the envelopes also indicate a remark-
able lack of concern for their archival value, in that one or more
of their custodians have torn off the stamps!

Most of the letters were from London, but several came
from elsewhere in Britain—two were written by a woman in
Bradford who was actually caught and charged. Some came
from abroad, including one from Philadelphia, USA, one from
France, one from Portugal and a few from Ireland. Several
were not posted but were found in the street, or in one case
tacked to a tree; one was washed up on a beach in Kent in a bottle. Most were sent to the police, sometimes to a named officer,
though others were addressed to newspapers. A few were sent
anonymously to members of the public; two of these were sent
to her neighbours as 'a lark' by a woman from near Aberdare in
south Wales, an act which backfired when the magistrate
threatened to commit her to the assizes for trial.

Several letters were sent to George Lusk, who had received
a great deal of personal publicity through the activities of the
Whitechapel Vigilance Committee. And in one of them the threat

made in many of the others was carried out—to enclose a human body part. This famous letter, the original of which is now missing though it is known in facsimile and quoted in a report written by Donald Swanson (HO 144/221/A49301C), differed from the others in another way too: it is one of the relatively few not signed 'Jack the Ripper' (see plate 17). The letter arrived in the late afternoon of 16 October 1888 in a small cardboard box with a smudged and illegible postmark. With it was half a kidney. Headed 'from hell', the letter read:

> Mr Lusk Sor I send you half the kidne I took from one woman prasarved it for you tother piece I fried and ate it was very nise. I may send you the bloody knif that took it out if you only wate a whil longer. Signed Catch me when you can Mishter Lusk.

Lusk's first instinct was to throw the kidney away in disgust, but fellow committee members urged him to show it to a medical man. A local doctor's assistant confirmed that it was human, and it was taken to the London Hospital. There the pathological curator of the museum, Dr Thomas Openshaw, examined it and stated that it was half a left human kidney, but that he could deduce little more because it had been preserved in spirits. This did not deter the press from claiming that he had pronounced it as belonging to a woman who had died within the last three weeks and who had been a heavy drinker. The obvious conclusion was reached: this was part of the kidney that had been removed from Catherine Eddowes, and it must therefore have been the murderer himself who had sent it to George Lusk.

Openshaw himself then received a letter, postmarked London 29 October (see plate 18):

> Old boss you was rite it was the left kidney i was goin to hop-
> perate agin close to your ospitle just as i was goin to dror mi
> nife along of er bloomin throte them cusses of coppers spoilt
> the game but i guess i wil be on the job soon and will send you
> another bit of innerds jack the ripper
>
> Have you seen the devle with his mikerscope and scalpel a
> lookin at a kidney with a slide cocked up. (MEPO 3/3157)

The attitude of the police to the Lusk letter and kidney can be deduced from the report submitted on 27 October 1888 to the Home Office by Inspector James McWilliam of the City Police (HO 144/221/A49301C; the destruction of the City Police records in the Blitz means that little is known about their investigation of the Eddowes murder, but this report survived among Home Office papers). After suggesting that publicity should not be given to the doctor's opinion that it was a human kidney—in vain, it seems, as the story had already been splashed all over the papers—McWilliam commented that 'It might turn out after all to be the act of a medical student who would have no difficulty in obtaining the organ in question.'

A real communication from the murderer, with a body part from Eddowes, or a gruesome practical joke by a medical student? Whichever was the case, the police were no nearer catching the killer. Yet it was not for lack of trying. McWilliam's report details persistent and wide-ranging attempts to find him. A priority had been to locate Eddowes' husband, Thomas Conway, after her daughter testified at the inquest that she had lost touch with her father. The only fact known about him was that he had served in the army and was in receipt of a pension, but no one of his name could be found in army records. Yet the police finally managed it. As McWilliam reported: 'Considerable difficulty was experienced in finding Conway in consequence of his having enlisted in the name of Thomas Quinn; he was found however, also the three children and two sisters of the deceased.' McWilliam also revealed that he had sent officers 'to all the lunatic asylums in London to make enquiry respecting persons recently admitted or discharged: many persons being of opinion that these crimes are of too revolting a character to have been committed by a sane person.' Huge efforts were being expended in the search, but it was all proving futile; the police reports exude frustration.

The press meanwhile continued to castigate the Home Secretary, Henry Matthews. A testy memo from him in response to McWilliam's report, preserved in the same Home Office file and dated 30 October 1888, betrays all too clearly his annoyance at the lack of progress:

> This report tells very little... The City Police are wholly 'at fault' as regards the detection of the murders. The word on the wall was 'Jewes' not 'Juwes'. This is important: unless it was a

clerical error [here there is a rather pained marginal note from Godfrey Lushington, Permanent Under Secretary, reading 'Not so I believe GL']... The printed report of the inquest contains much more information than this. They evidently want to tell us nothing [another marginal note from GL: 'I don't think so.']

The civil servants were clearly having to mediate between their irritable boss and the hard-pressed police. Lushington's advice at the end of the memo to Charles Murdoch, the Home Office clerk dealing with the matter, was that it was inadvisable to approach the police directly with some of Matthews' ill-informed and pointless questions: 'when Mr Matthews comes to town I would advise that he should ask Sir J Fraser [City Police Commissioner] to come to the HO. He will then have full particulars.' Reading between the lines, it seems that Matthews' staff shared at least some of the public and press reservations about the Home Secretary and his efficacy in this case.

The 'double event' had taken place on the last day of September. The whole of October had now passed without any further murders. Fuelled by news that similar murders had been committed in other parts of Britain, including Manchester and Gateshead, speculation arose that the killer had left London. The early November issue of the American journal *Littell's Living Age* chronicles the reviving spirits of Whitechapel:

A little way down out of the public house glare, and Buck's Row looks to be a singularly desolate, out-of-the-way region. But there is a piano-organ grinding out the 'Men of Harlech' over the spot where the murdered woman was found; women and girls are freely coming and going through the darkness, and the rattle of sewing-machines, and the rushing of railway trains, and the noisy horseplay of a gang of boys, all seem to be combining with the organ-grinder to drown recollection and to banish all unpleasant reflection. 'There seems to be little apprehension of further mischief by this assassin at large,' was an observation addressed to a respectable-looking elderly man within a few yards of the house in Hanbury Street, where the latest victim was found [*sic*]. 'No; very little. People, most of 'em, think he's gone to Gateshead,' was the reply.

They were false hopes. On 9 November 1888, the police informed the Home Office that another murder had been committed.

FOULEST MURDER

A note timed 12.30 from Sir Charles Warren to Godfrey Lushington reads 'Mutilated dead body of woman reported to be found this morning inside room of house in Dorset Street Spitalfields. Information just received' (HO 144/221/A49301F). A more formal letter followed, together with a memo saying 'I have asked Commissioner by telephone to inform HO as soon as possible of any further information which may reach him in the case.' The final communication is a small piece of paper with a pencilled note across the top, 'Telephone message from Police

9.11.88'. This is perhaps the only mention in the Ripper files of the telephone being used as a mode of swift communication; the police force involved must have been stirred up like a hive of bees. Beneath is written in pen: 'Body is believed to be that of a prostitute much mutilated. Dr Bond is at present engaged in making his examination—but his report has not yet been received. Full report cannot be furnished until medical officers have completed enquiries.'

The victim was Mary Jane Kelly, a prostitute aged 25, whose body was found at 10.45 am in a room she rented at 13 Miller's Court, Dorset Street, Spitalfields. Dr Thomas Bond's report of what he found at the crime scene and of his post-mortem examination—one of the long-missing documents returned anonymously to Scotland Yard in 1987—makes horrific reading:

> The body was lying naked in the middle of the bed... The whole of the surface of the abdomen & thighs was removed & the abdominal cavity emptied of its viscera. The breasts were cut off, the arms mutilated by several jagged wounds & the face hacked beyond recognition of the features. The tissues of the neck were severed all round down to the bone. The viscera were found in various parts viz: the uterus & kidneys with one breast under the head, the other breast by the rt foot, the liver between the feet, the intestines by the right side & the spleen by the left side of the body. The flaps removed from the abdomen and thighs were on a table. The bed clothing at the right corner was saturated with blood, & on the floor beneath was a pool of blood covering about 2 feet square. The wall by

the right side of the bed & in a line with the neck was marked
by blood which had struck it in a number of separate splashes.

Bond's examination further revealed that the killer had cut off
part of his victim's nose, cheeks, eyebrows and ears and had
slashed her throat right down to the vertebrae of the spine. He
had removed large flaps of flesh from the abdomen and thighs
and had cut off both breasts with circular incisions, and
removed her heart.

The inquest opened on the Monday after the murder, 12
November. The first witness was Joseph Barnett, a labourer
and porter, who testified that he had lived with Kelly for a year
and eight months. He had left at the end of October 'because
she had a woman of bad character there, whom she took in out
of compassion, and I objected to it'. They had nevertheless
parted on good terms. He now chillingly told the coroner, 'I
have seen the body, and I identify it by the ear and eyes, which
are all that I can recognize; but I am positive it is the same
woman I knew.'

Kelly had told him that she had been born in Limerick, but
had moved to Wales when very young and married a collier who
was subsequently killed in a pit explosion. She had then gone to
Cardiff to a cousin who, according to Barnett, led her into bad
ways and was 'the cause of her downfall'. She decided to call herself Marie Jeanette after a brief trip to France, and had lived in
various 'gay houses' in London before meeting and moving in
with Barnett. He told the court that she did sometimes drink

too much, but that when they were together she was generally quiet and sober.

The body had been found by Thomas Bowyer, an employee of John McCarthy, grocer and owner of the lodging house where Kelly lived. He had been ordered by his boss to go to Kelly's room that morning to collect overdue rent. When there was no answer to his knock at the door, he looked through the window and saw the horrors inside:

> I put my hand through the broken pane and lifted the curtain. I saw two pieces of flesh lying on the table... The second time I looked I saw a body on the bed, and blood on the floor. I at once went very quietly to Mr McCarthy... We both went to the police station, but first of all we went to the window, and McCarthy looked in to satisfy himself... The inspector returned with us.

McCarthy corroborated his employee's evidence, adding that the rent for the room was 4s 6d a week and that Kelly was 29s in arrears. He had, he said, 'frequently seen the deceased the worse for drink. When sober she was an exceptionally quiet woman, but when in drink she had more to say.'

According to another witness, she had been drunk on the night of her death. Mary Ann Cox, a fellow prostitute who lived in a nearby room at the lodging house, testified: 'I last saw her alive on Thursday night, at a quarter to twelve, very much intoxicated. [She was with] a short, stout man, shabbily dressed. He had on a longish coat, very shabby, and carried a pot of ale in his hand…' Cox described him further as having a round hard billycock hat, a shaven chin, a blotchy face and a full carroty moustache. She had called out 'Goodnight' to Kelly, who answered her and said 'I am going to have a song.' She was still singing at 1 am when Cox returned after going out for an hour, but all was quiet and dark when she returned after a further foray on to the streets at 3 am.

The police did not enter Kelly's room until 1.30 pm on the day of her death. They were waiting for bloodhounds to arrive, and it was only when Superintendent Arnold came and told them that the order to deploy the dogs had been counter-manded that they forced the door. Inspector Abberline was on the scene; as he testified:

> I took an inventory of the contents of the room. There were
> traces of a large fire having been kept up in the grate, so much
> so that it had melted the spout of a kettle off. We have since
> gone through the ashes in the fireplace; there were remnants of
> clothing, a portion of a brim of a hat, and a skirt, and it
> appeared as if a large quantity of women's clothing had been
> burnt… I can only imagine that [the fire] was to make a light
> for the man to see what he was doing. There was only one small
> candle in the room, on the top of a broken wine-glass.

Oddly, there was an element of doubt about the time of death—as there was about the identification of the victim. A witness at the inquest claimed to have seen Kelly at around 8 am, standing in the street looking ill after vomiting in the gutter, and

Maurice Lewis, a tailor, later told the press that he too had seen her at around 10 am that morning. But the inquest itself was brief, and the verdict the predictable one of 'wilful murder against some person or persons unknown'.

The mutilations carried out on Kelly's body were horrendous. This time, uniquely, the murderer had no need to hurry or fear being disturbed. Within the privacy of his victim's room he had butchered her at leisure and—presumably—indulged to the full his escalating blood lust. Whether or not he had been away, as so many East Enders had fondly hoped, the killer was now back with a vengeance.

The police still resisted the idea of a reward. But there had been debate about whether offering a pardon to accomplices not directly involved might smoke out someone with guilty knowledge of the crimes and their perpetrator. Such a person was unlikely to come forward under threat of the hangman's noose, so now the highest in the land took a hand in the case. On the day after the murder, a letter from Sir Charles Warren announced, 'The Cabinet have decided to offer today a pardon to anyone but the actual murderers in the case that occurred yesterday.'

The idea of a pardon had also occurred to a member of the public called James Frederick Brooks, but this time with a twist in its tail. As he wrote to the authorities on 16 November, 'I propose as a necessity of exception to offer a pardon to the perpetrator of these dreadful deeds and if captured give him his deserts and for once break our national word of honour for the benefit of the universe' (HO 144/221/A49301C).

Other correspondents made suggestions of variable value. J. Smith from Burnham, Essex, wrote on 10 November:

> I beg to remind you that flogging stopped garrotting. If the culprit could be assured that in addition to the penalty of hanging, he will previously if found guilty have as much of the cat as human nature (and as often for one twelve months) can bear, his or her craven heart would quake. Nothing of less justice will stop it. (HO 144/221/A49301C)

Perhaps more useful—and certainly less cruel—was the suggestion from Thomas Blair of Dumfries that 12 men be selected 'of short stature, and as far as possible of effeminate appearance, but of known courage and tried nerve' to dress as 'females of the class from whom the victims are selected' and then used to lure the murderer into a trap. He stressed that it would have to be done in absolute secrecy in case the press got hold of the plan, and pointed out with reason that these men 'would require to have all their wits about them'.

News of the latest murder was rapidly conveyed round the country and the world. By 10 November it had reached all over North America and as far as Australia and New Zealand. At home, the newspapers carried long, detailed accounts of Kelly's terrible wounds, as well as angry castigation of senior police and the Home Secretary. A leader in the *Daily Telegraph* of 10 November, while bemoaning the lack of results, refused to blame ordinary policemen who

> have never had, and they have not now, any firmer friends or
> warmer advocates than ourselves. They are not highly paid,
> and they are not drawn from a class generally educated to the
> exercise of authority, of patience, or of discipline; yet, as a body,
> they have for years past displayed all these qualities in ample
> measure, and have thereby earned the respect—we might
> almost say the friendship—of the people.

The same could not be said of Henry Matthews or Sir Charles
Warren. Of the latter—a military man in an unfamiliar role—it
was claimed that 'He has abounded in the qualities which it was
desirable that he should possess only in moderation, and he has
been signally lacking in qualities of which it is impossible to
have too much. The result is failure.'

Robert Anderson, Assistant Commissioner (Crime) of the
Met, now asked Dr Thomas Bond, who had carried out the
post-mortem on Mary Jane Kelly, to take an overview of the
medical evidence in the last five cases, and specifically to give
his opinion on whether the killer possessed surgical skill and
anatomical knowledge. Dr Bond's report (MEPO 3/141) is worth
quoting at length (see also p. 4):

1   All five murders were no doubt committed by the same hand.
    In the first four the throats appear to have been cut from
    left to right. In the last case owing to the extensive mutila-
    tion it is impossible to say in what direction the fatal cut was
    made, but arterial blood was found on the wall in splashes

I was not codging
dear old Boss when
I gave you that tip
you ll hear about
saucy Jacky s work
tomorrow double
event this time
number one squealed
a bit couldnt
finish straight
off. had not time
to get ears for
police. thanks for
keeping last letter
back till I got
to work again.
Jack the Ripper

13 *Left*: The 'saucy Jacky' postcard, smeared with blood and postmarked 1 October, the day after the Stride and Eddowes killings; this was the second 'Jack the Ripper' missive.

14 *Below*: a 'self-portrait' from one of many subsequent hoax letters signed 'Jack the Ripper'. The accompanying text reads: 'This is my photo of Jack the Ripper 10 more and up goes the sponge'. (MEPO 3/142)

15 *Above*: Vigilantes on the streets of the East End; from the *Illustrated London News* of 13 October 1888. (ZPER 34/93)

16 *Right*: The police notice requesting information on the murders; such initiatives encouraged public involvement in the crimes. (MEPO 3/140)

17 *Opposite*: The 'Lusk letter', sent with half a human kidney to George Lusk of the Whitechapel Vigilance Committee; it is one of the few letters not signed 'Jack the Ripper'.

POLICE NOTICE.

TO THE OCCUPIER.

On the mornings of Friday, 31st August, Saturday 8th, and Sunday, 30th September, 1888, Women were murdered in or near Whitechapel, supposed by some one residing in the immediate neighbourhood. Should you know of any person to whom suspicion is attached, you are earnestly requested to communicate at once with the nearest Police Station.

Metropolitan Police Office,
30th September, 1888.

Printed by M'Corquodale & Co. Limited, "The Armoury," Southwark.

From hell

Mr Lusk

Sor

I send you half the
Kidne I took from one women
prasarved it for you tother piece
I fried and ate it was very nise I
may send you the bloody knif that
took it out if you only wate a whil
longer

Signed   Catch me when
you Can
Mishter Lusk —

Old boss you was rite it was
the left Kidny i was goin to
hoperate agin close to your
ospitte just as i was goin
to dror mi nife along of
er bloomen throte them
cusses of coppers spoilt
the game but i guess i wil
be on the job soon and will
send you another bit of
innerds   jack the ripper

O have you seen the devle
with his mikerocope and scalpul
a lookin at a kidney
with a slide cocked up

18 *Opposite*: The letter purporting to be from the Ripper received by Dr Thomas Openshaw, who examined the human kidney sent to George Lusk. (MEPO 3/3157)

19 *Below*: One of several hoax letters addressed to Sir Charles Warren, found pinned to a passage wall in Bethnal Green. (MEPO 3/142)

20 *Below right*: Sir Charles Warren; his conduct of the case attracted a great deal of criticism, particularly his decision to sponge away the Goulston Street inscription before it could be photographed. (COPY 1/443)

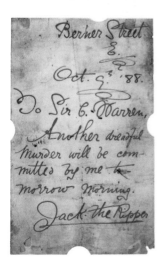

21 *Above*: The cover of the *Illustrated Police News* of 17 November 1888, with a drawing of Mary Jane Kelly and several vignettes of the murder scene.

22 *Above right*: The *Illustrated Police News* of 24 November 1888 carried this artist's impression of the man Hutchinson had seen with Mary Jane Kelly before her death.

Metropolitan Police.

No. 6.

Special Report.

H Division.

12th November 1888

Reference to Report:
Continued

stern. They both went into Dorset
Street I followed them. they both
stood at the Corner of the Court for
about 3 minutes. He said something
to her. she said alright my dear
come along you will be comfortable
He then placed his arm on her shoulder
and gave her a kiss. She said she had
lost her handkerchief. he then pulled
his handkerchief a red one out and
gave it to her. they both then went up
the Court together. I then went to the
Court to see if I could see them but
could not. I stood there for about
three quarters of an hour. to see if they
came out they did not so I went away

Circulated
to A.S.

Description age about 34 or 35. high 5 ft 6
complexion pale. dark eyes and eye lashes
dark slight moustache. curled up each
end. and hair dark. very surley looking
dress long. dark. coat. collar and cuffs
trimmed astracan. and a dark jacket
under. light waistcoat. dark trousers
dark felt hat turned down in the middle.
button boots. and gaiters. with white
buttons. wore a very thick gold chain.
white linen collar. black tie with horse
shoe pin. respectable appearance

George Hutchinson

---

23 *Above*: The second page of Inspector Abberline's report on George Hutchinson's witness statement after the Kelly murder, with the detailed description he provided. (MEPO 3/140)

24 *Left*: George Chapman, aka Severin Klosowski, who was Abberline's chief suspect; he was hanged in 1903 for poisoning his three wives.

25 *Below*: Montague Druitt, one of three men named by Melville Macnaghten as a Ripper suspect; his body was found in the Thames at the end of December 1888 and had been several weeks in the water.

close to where the woman's head must have been lying.

2   All the circumstances surrounding the murders lead me to form the opinion that the women must have been lying down when murdered and in every case the throat was first cut.

3   In the four murders of which I have seen the notes only, I cannot form a very definite opinion as to the time that had elapsed between the murder and the discovery of the body. In one case, that of Berner Street, the discovery appears to have been immediately after the deed. In Buck's Row, Hanbury Street and Mitre Square three or four hours only could have elapsed. In the Dorset Street case … it is pretty certain that the woman must have been dead about 12 hours & the partly digested food would indicate that death took place about 3 or 4 hours after the food was taken, so one or 2 o'clock in the morning would be the probable time of the murder.

4   In all the cases there appears to be no evidence of struggling and the attacks were probably so sudden and made in such a position that the woman could neither resist nor cry out. In the Dorset Street case the corner of the sheet to the right of the woman's head was much cut & saturated with blood, indicating that the face may have been covered with the sheet at the time of the attack.

5   In the four first cases the murderer must have attacked from the right side of the victim. In the Dorset Street case, he must have attacked from in front or from the left, as there would be no room for him between the wall and the part of the bed on which the woman was lying. Again the

blood had flowed down on the right side of the woman and spurted on to the wall.

6   The murderer would not necessarily be splashed or deluged with blood, but his hands & arms must have been covered & parts of his clothing must certainly have been smeared with blood.

7   The mutilations in each case excepting the Berner Street one were all of the same character and shewed clearly that in all the murders the object was mutilation.

8   In each case the mutilation was inflicted by a person who had no scientific nor anatomical knowledge. In my opinion he does not even possess the technical knowledge of a butcher or a horse slaughterer or any person accustomed to cut up dead animals.

9   The instrument must have been a strong knife at least six inches long, very sharp, pointed at the top and about an inch in width. It may have been a clasp knife, a butcher's knife or a surgeon's knife. I think it was no doubt a straight knife.

There had now been six killings in a little over three months: six women violently done to death with a knife, in what appears to have been an escalating cycle of furious blood lust. Yet there was not the slightest clue as to who had done these dreadful deeds. He had a name—but the man who really was Jack the Ripper remained in the shadows.

CHAPTER FOUR

Hunted and Hunters

There were several witnesses who may have set eyes on Jack the Ripper. Elizabeth Long had seen a man with Annie Chapman outside the door to 29 Hanbury Street 40 minutes before her body was found—but only his back. PC Smith and Israel Schwartz had both witnessed Elizabeth Stride talking to a man in Berner Street half an hour before she met her death— but in the darkness of a rainy night. The men hurrying home through Mitre Square that same night took little notice of the man and woman on the corner of a passage leading into the square; one of them said he doubted that he would recognize the man again although he had been facing him, and he was not curious enough to look back to see what the couple were doing. Frustratingly, the descriptions these casual witnesses gave of the man they had seen differed in almost every respect from each other, although they all agreed that he was wearing dark clothing.

However, in the Kelly case there was a credible witness who claimed that he would know the man again. George Hutchinson presented himself at Commercial Road police station on 12

November 1888 and was interviewed by Inspector Abberline
(see plate 23). He told the inspector that over the three years or
so he had known Kelly he had occasionally given her a few
shillings, and that at about 2 am on the night of her death he
had met her in the street and she had asked for sixpence. He
had no money to offer her, so she said goodbye to him and went
off towards Thrawl Street:

> A man coming in the opposite direction tapped her on the
> shoulder and said something to her they both burst out laugh-
> ing. I heard her say alright to him and the man said you will be
> alright for what I have told you. He then placed his right hand
> around her shoulders. He also had a kind of a small parcel in his
> left hand with a kind of a strap round it. I stood against the
> lamp of the Queens Head public house and watched him. They
> both then came past me and the man hung down his head with
> his hat over his eyes. I stooped down and looked him in the
> face. (MEPO 3/140)

Because Hutchinson knew Kelly, he carried on watching the
pair for several minutes, and when they went into the court
where she lived, he stood around for three-quarters of an hour
to see if they came out again. As Inspector Abberline said in his
report, 'he was surprised to see a man so well dressed in her
company which caused him to watch them'.

Well dressed he certainly was. According to Hutchinson, the
man was wearing

> a long dark coat, collar and cuffs trimmed astracan [*sic*], and a

dark jacket under. Light waistcoat, dark trousers, dark felt hat
turned down in the middle, button boots and gaiters with white
buttons, wore a very thick gold chain, white linen collar, black
tie with horse shoe pin, respectable appearance.

He further described him as 'about 34 or 35, height 5ft 6in, complexion pale, dark eyes and eyelashes, slight moustache curled
up each end and hair dark. Very surly looking ... walked very
sharp, Jewish appearance.'

The last words of Hutchinson's statement were 'can be identified'. So the police immediately arranged for him to be accompanied round the district by two officers in the hope that he
might see the man again. The description appeared in the press,
and a drawing based on it was published in the 24 November
issue of *Illustrated Police News*, which in fact had no connection with the police (see plate 22). But once again, nothing came
of what must have seemed a hopeful breakthrough.

The cover of the 17 November issue of *Illustrated Police
News* had been given over to lurid drawings of the Kelly murder, dominated by the victim as she had been in life and with
several vignettes of scenes in her drama (see plate 21). Two of
these drawings featured the mutilated woman lying on her bed.
Kelly was described as the seventh victim, though the otherwise useful map provided of the murder locations wrongly identified Goulston Street as the place where she met her death,
and also failed to provide a location for the first of the series.
Clearly there was still little known about the Smith murder,

although it was now being touted as the first Ripper crime.

Letters from 'Jack the Ripper' had continued to flood in throughout October. Now the Kelly murder gave fresh impetus to the correspondence. Comparison had been drawn between the London murders and a series of similar crimes in Texas. These had now ceased, and there was much speculation that the Texas killer had moved on to Whitechapel. There were also threats that the killer had crossed the Atlantic in the other direction: a letter from Philadelphia threatened 'when I have the lay of the locality I might take a notion to do a little ripping there'. The hint of Americanism in the 'Dear Boss' letter had clearly not gone unnoticed, for an American theme was not uncommon in others. One correspondent claimed that he was killing women in London because he had lent money to three English girls in San Francisco who had absconded back to England without repaying him.

Several of the letters written towards the end of October, before the Kelly murder, indirectly commented on that month's lull by claiming that the writer was ill or had been away, and that he would soon be at his work again, while one posted after Kelly's murder, on 19 November, included a self-portrait in an astrakhan-trimmed coat with the message, 'I am Jack the Ripper catch me if you can shall have one in Woolwhich this week look out for me at Woolwhich'. Though most of the letters restricted themselves to vague promises of more 'ripping' to come, one chose instead to comment on the correspondence generally. Dated 10 November, the day after the Kelly murder, it is written in capitals and reads:

> Well you see I've kept my word, and done for the one I said I would. I suppose you took no notice of what I said. Those other letters were not written by me at all and has [*sic*] some one has been kind enough to give me the name of 'Jack the Ripper' I'll accept it and act up to it. Look out for the next. P.S. You can't trace me by this writing so its no use on the police stations.

It was clear that the deluded time-wasting was unabated.

In addition to the Ripper letters the police and the press continued to be inundated throughout October and November with comments, theories and advice from members of the public. A trawl through *The Times* and the *Daily Telegraph* for 5 October provides rich evidence of this. A letter in *The Times* suggested that the murderer had a financial motive: to kill until a reward was offered, and then to frame an innocent man and collect the money. The *Daily Telegraph* published an article summarizing all the comments received from its correspondents, including one who firmly believed that no one could be so depraved as to write the letters—so they must be from the killer himself. Several others in the same edition expressed their pity and concern for the 'wretched women of the East End', and a kindly man from Leyton was full of disgust and pity that Eddowes had been sent adrift from the police station in the early hours and into the hands of her killer:

> If it had been a respectable person, who had taken an extra
> glass, she would have been retained until about eight or nine
> o'clock, and fined for being drunk and incapable. But in this
> case it is a poor creature without a cent in her pocket towards
> payment of a fine, and she must suffer, being sent away imme-
> diately she is sober. If she had been retained ... she could not
> have met with her death.

A rather tongue-in-cheek *Daily Telegraph* leader, also on 5
October, commented on the activities of the Whitechapel Vigilance Committee:

> Shortly before twelve o'clock these assassin-hunters are
> despatched upon their mission. Their footfall is silenced by the
> use of goloshes, and their own safety is assured by the carrying
> of police-whistles and stout sticks...

Some correspondents detected clues in the Ripper's handwriting. One was sure that 'the writing is a decided Civil Service
hand', another that 'the writer is an American'. Fish-cleaning,
pig-sticking, slaughtering—all were suggested as likely trades
for the killer, while other correspondents wanted the sewers to
be thoroughly searched on the grounds that the miscreant could
both escape through them and use them to hide his bloody
clothing. One who signed himself 'Bloodhound' commented:

> I have had a large practical acquaintance with homicidal
> maniacs, for I have lived with them, and I emphatically assert
> that this series of crimes is the work of no lunatic, homicidal or
> otherwise. There is too much coherence of idea, too much fixity

> of purpose, too much self-control displayed… These atrocities
> are the handiwork of no individual, but of a confederacy.

The timing of the murders offered further food for thought. Martha Tabram had been killed on the night of a bank holiday and the others met their deaths in the early mornings of two Fridays, a Saturday and two Sundays. This led to the reasonable suspicion that the killer might have been in London only at weekends, and might therefore be someone in a regular line of work which took up his time during the week or perhaps took him away for days on end. One E.K. Larkins became convinced that the murderer was a cattleman from Oporto in Portugal: in January 1889 he sent the police a seven-page report on his observation of ships' traffic between Portugal and the London docks, and his enquiries into those on board. The police had, however, already followed up this idea, finding that no one man had served on each of the ships that were in port in London at the crucial times. Larkins was not deterred. He deduced from this that several individuals were guilty of the Ripper crimes, and as late as January 1893 wrote about the matter again to Herbert Asquith, now Home Secretary (HO 144/221/A49301C).

FRESH BLOOD

After Mary Jane Kelly's death in early November 1888, the East End enjoyed a lull like that in October—until a killing in

Poplar on 20 December aroused fears that the Ripper was back. However, Rose Mylett had been strangled, not stabbed, and her body was not mutilated; she had also been seen arguing with two sailors who were potentially in the frame for her death.

There followed another quiet period. Then, in July 1889, Alice McKenzie was found in Castle Alley, Whitechapel, with her throat cut and her abdomen mutilated with knife wounds. Dr George Baxter Phillips, the police surgeon who examined the body, did not believe that this was the work of the Ripper. The wounds to her throat and the knife stabbings on her body were very different from those inflicted on the 1888 victims, while the cuts on the abdomen were quite superficial. It was his view—and the coroner's—that this was a copycat murder, by someone perhaps less bold with his knife. Dr Thomas Bond, who performed a second post-mortem, disagreed. He reported that the stomach cuts, as in the previous cases, indicated a sexual subtext which might argue for a link.

But once again there were no suspects. A man named William Brodie confessed, but his meandering statement was confused—'I then went to Lands End in Cornwall, but I only stayed there about ten minutes. I walked there and back in half an hour or three quarters... I returned into Whitechapel through an avenue of trees from the forest'—and no blood was found on his clothing. As Superintendent Arnold commented, 'He appears of unsound mind and I do not think any reliance can be placed upon his statement'. (MEPO 3/140)

Two months later, on 10 September 1889, the torso of a woman who remains unidentified to this day was found under a railway arch in Pinchin Street, Whitechapel. The head and legs were missing, and it was clear that she had been dismembered and moved from the place where she met her death—probably the murderer's home, and probably a couple of days before her remains were found. James Monro, who by this time was Commissioner of the Metropolitan Police, himself investigated this case. He came to the conclusion that—although it was possible that the body had been left in Whitechapel in order to suggest a link—'this case is not the work of the Ripper' (MEPO 3/140).

The whole of 1890 passed without any further violent deaths in Whitechapel. It was not until 13 February 1891 that there was another, which turned out to be the final killing in the series. This was the murder of Frances Coles, a prostitute found lying in the street at 2.15 am with her throat cut. This time there was a real suspect. Thomas Sadler, a sailor, admitted having consorted with Coles on several occasions, and his movements between ship and shore made him a credible possibility for the other deaths too. The man seen in Mitre Square with Catherine Eddowes had been described as having the appearance of a sailor, and Sadler was known to be of a violent disposition. There was a growing belief that at last Jack the Ripper was in custody. But exhaustive police enquiries into Sadler's movements eventually ruled him out, even from the Coles murder with which he had been charged. He was eventually released on

3 March 1891, though later that year he was bound over to keep the peace after his wife complained that he had threatened to kill her.

POLICE AND SUSPECTS

The documentation that has survived makes it abundantly clear that the police went to enormous lengths to catch the killer. They followed up every lead, however tenuous; they drafted in extra men who were to remain in Whitechapel on high alert for many months after the deaths appeared to have ceased; they tried out new ideas like the use of bloodhounds. By the time it seemed that there would be no more murders, and that the Ripper had left the scene in one way or another, the policemen most closely involved with the case must have been exhausted and deeply frustrated. Despite huge efforts on their part, and the massive outcry—as well as support—from the public, no one was found responsible for any of the Whitechapel murders.

The names of some of the police officers involved are known through their reports and through contemporary accounts of the murders and the investigations. Sir Charles Warren, Commissioner of the Metropolitan Police, is the senior officer who attracts most criticism, mainly because of his removal of the Goulston Street inscription and because he made enemies through his rigidly military approach to police work. One of those enemies was his Assistant Commissioner (CID), James Monro, who had resigned from the police in August 1888 after a disagreement with Warren over his attitude towards the CID (Warren favoured uniformed policing over detective work) and because Warren was blocking Monro's wish to appoint his friend, Melville Macnaghten, to a senior detective role. The Home Secretary, Henry Matthews, never a strong supporter of Warren, further undermined him by appointing Monro, after his resignation, as a sort of roving 'head of the detective service', an honorary position he held during that autumn of mayhem in Whitechapel. When Warren resigned on the day of the Kelly murder, Monro became his successor, and in June 1889 he made Macnaghten Assistant Chief Constable (CID).

The name of Chief Inspector Donald Swanson as overall supervisor of the enquiries often crops up in the documentation, as does that of Inspector Abberline, the officer perhaps most closely involved with the investigation through running the case day to day. Further down the ranks, the name of Detective Sergeant John Thicke—who arrested John Pizer, 'Leather Apron'—comes up more than once. Interestingly, he was himself named as a suspect by a member of the public. A Mr H.J. Haslewood of Tottenham wrote to the police on 10 September 1889 to say that he believed the murderer to be a policeman and that he would furnish a name provided his anonymity was assured. Haslewood then named 'Sergeant J Thicke, otherwise called "Johnny Upright"', and recommended that he should be watched. The police, naturally, treated this accusation as the work of someone with a grudge (HO 144/220/A49301).

Melville Macnaghten was not directly involved in the 1888 investigations, but he is the author of one of the most important documents in the Ripper archive—the so-called 'Macnaghten memorandum' (MEPO 3/141). Written on 23 February 1894, it summarizes the case and for the first time names the three most likely suspects. It appears to have been written in response to press speculation—which had recently been aired in the *Sun* newspaper—that a man called Thomas Cutbush, convicted in 1891 for minor knife attacks on two women and confined in an asylum, was the Whitechapel murderer.

Macnaghten was quite certain that the 'double event' of 30 September 1888 happened because the killer was disturbed in the middle of his first murder and so '"*nondum satiatus*" [not yet satiated] went in search of a further victim...' And, as the memo went on:

> It will be noticed that the fury of the mutilations increased in each case, and, seemingly, the appetite only became sharpened by indulgence. It seems, then, highly improbable that the murderer would have suddenly stopped in November '88, and been content to recommence operations by merely prodding a girl behind some two years and four months afterwards. A much more rational theory is that the murderer's brain gave way altogether after his awful glut in Miller's Court, and that he immediately committed suicide, or, as a possible alternative,

was found to be so hopelessly mad by his relations that he was by them confined in some asylum.

Macnaghten clearly gave little credibility to the witnesses who claimed to have seen the killer, because he went on to say, 'No one ever saw the Whitechapel murderer; many homicidal maniacs were suspected, but no shadow of proof could be thrown on any one.' He then listed three suspects:

A Mr M.J. Druitt [see plate 25], said to be a doctor and of good family, who disappeared at the time of the Miller's Court murder, and whose body (which was said to have been upwards of a month in the water) was found in the Thames on 31 December, or about seven weeks after that murder. He was sexually insane and from private inf. I have little doubt but that his own family believed him to have been the murderer.

Kosminski, a Polish Jew and resident in Whitechapel. This man became insane owing to many years indulgence in solitary vices. He had a great hatred of women, specially of the prostitute class, and had strong homicidal tendencies; he was removed to a lunatic asylum about March 1889. There were many circs. connected with this man which made him a strong 'suspect'.

Michael Ostrog, a Russian doctor, and a convict, who was subsequently detained in a lunatic asylum as a homicidal maniac. This man's antecedents were of the worst possible type, and his whereabouts at the time of the murders could never be ascertained.

The main aim of the Macnaghten memorandum was to dispel the press accusations about Thomas Cutbush; the memo specifically says 'I may mention the cases of three men any one of whom would have been more likely than Cutbush to have committed this series of murders.' It is therefore arguable that these possibilities were simply plucked out of a hat to illustrate the fact that there were many stronger suspects available, and that these three men were not necessarily the prime contenders. However, this memo is the first police document to offer any names at all.

And there are tantalizing hints from memoirs and interviews that some of the policemen involved believed they knew the Ripper's identity. Robert Anderson was quoted in press interviews as suspecting three unnamed men, who were then identified as Macnaghten's three. It later emerged that his strongest suspect was Aaron Kosminski—a view confirmed when Chief Inspector Swanson's personal copy of Anderson's memoir, *The Lighter Side of My Official Life*, was donated to the Metropolitan Police Crime Museum. Anderson had written that it was 'a definitely ascertainable fact' that the killer was a Polish Jew, and that 'the only person who ever had a good view of the murderer unhesitatingly identified the suspect the instant he was confronted with him'. A marginal note initialled by Swanson was found in the book, indicating that the witness refused to testify because he was reluctant to send a fellow Jew to the gallows. The so-called 'Swanson's marginalia' added that 'Kosminski was the suspect.' It is thought that this confrontation between suspect and witness took place in an asylum in Brighton, and that the witness was either Israel Schwartz, who had seen Elizabeth Stride being attacked, or Joseph Lawende, who had seen Catherine Eddowes with a man in Mitre Square.

Inspector Abberline took a different tack. He apparently believed that George Chapman, also known as Severin Klosowski, was the Ripper (see plate 24). Klosowski had been apprenticed to a surgeon in Poland before coming to England, had lived in Whitechapel at the crucial time, and had been in America when a series of apparently similar murders and mutilations occurred. He was eventually found guilty of murdering his three wives by poison, and hanged in April 1903.

A further name emerged from the so-called 'Littlechild letter'. Dated 23 September 1913, this was sent by ex-Chief Inspector John Littlechild to George Sims, who had written extensively about the Ripper murders in the *Sunday Referee* under the pseudonym 'Dagonet'. It is clear from Sims' articles that he believed firmly that Montague Druitt was Jack the Ripper, which was presumably the initial reason for the correspondence between the two of them. Oddly, given that he was a former member of the London police force, Littlechild professed in his letter never to have heard of 'Dr D. [Druitt]'. But at any event he went on to tell Sims:

amongst the suspects, and to my mind a very likely one, was a Dr T. (which sounds much like D.) He was an American quack named Tumblety and was at one time a frequent visitor to London and on these occasions constantly brought under the notice of police, there being a large dossier concerning him at Scotland Yard... Tumblety was arrested at the time of the murders in connection with unnatural offences and charged at Marlborough Street, remanded on bail, jumped his bail, and got away to Boulogne. He shortly left Boulogne and was never heard of afterwards. It was believed he committed suicide...

In fact, Tumblety had not committed suicide but had returned to America. He was watched by the police there—amid intense public speculation that he was the Whitechapel murderer—but never apprehended or charged. The full text of the Littlechild letter can be read on the Casebook website (see Sources & Reading).

As well as Chapman/Klosowski—whose method of murder, slow poison, could not have been more different from the Ripper's *modus operandi*—other men hanged for murder around the time of the Whitechapel events were investigated as potential suspects. In one case, that of William Bury who was executed in Dundee in April 1889 for the murder of his wife, Inspector Abberline was even sent to Scotland to investigate a possible link. Bury had strangled his wife and then stabbed her in the stomach, and it was reported that the words 'Jack the Ripper is in this sellar [*sic*]' had been found scrawled on the door of his apartment.

Another suspect, Frederick Deeming, was hanged in Australia in May 1892. The Australian police had found his wife's dead body under the floorboards of a house where he had previously lived, and police back in Liverpool subsequently discovered the bodies of his former wife and four children, their throats cut, concealed in another previous residence. Deeming had apparently lived in the East End of London at the time of the murders, and was said to have told his fellow inmates in Australia that he was the Ripper.

Yet another possibility was Neill Cream, hanged for murder in November 1892—but suspected solely on the basis that his executioner later swore he had uttered the words 'I am Jack...' just as the trap fell. In fact, Cream had been in prison in America at the time of the Ripper killings. Other unlikely names were bandied about at the time too—including the Duke of Clarence, known as Prince Eddy, oldest son of the Prince of Wales and second in line to the throne.

A recent addition to the list of suspects is James Maybrick, who died of arsenic poisoning in May 1889 and whose wife, Florence, was tried and condemned to death for his murder, though her sentence was commuted to life imprisonment. Maybrick's diaries, in which he confessed to being Jack the Ripper, emerged in 1992 in the possession of Michael Barrett, and have excited frenzied debate ever since. Tests on the ink, combined with internal inaccuracies and inconsistencies in facts about the crimes, have led most Ripperologists to dismiss the diaries as a forgery. And Barrett himself has admitted creating them—though he has also withdrawn this admission.

Whether or not one of the three Macnaghten suspects was

Jack the Ripper, it is clear that at least some of the police officers involved believed that the killer had stopped his blood-thirsty spree after the Kelly murder and that he was either dead or in an asylum. Macnaghten commented on the escalating scale of the violence perpetrated on the victims' bodies, concluding that the murderer must have been a maniac of the worst kind, and that after his final satiation he could well have committed suicide. Yet a letter dated 14 October 1896 seems to have caused a small flurry of alarm. Addressed to 'Dear Boss', and using the language of the original correspondence—'buckled', 'ha ha', 'yours truly'—it also (mis)quoted the Goulston Street inscription, and included the usual taunts: 'You police are a smart lot, the lot of you could nt catch one man Where have I been Dear Boss you d like to know. Abroad, if you would like to know, and just come back. ready to go on with my work and stop when you catch me'. The police went as far as making a comparison between its handwriting and that of earlier letters. The report on the letter by Chief Inspector Moore included the interesting comment that the Goulston Street writing was 'undoubtedly by the murderer'. But Superintendent Swanson concluded that 'the handwritings are not the same ... the letter may be put with other similar letters. Its circulation is to be regretted.' (MEPO 3/142)

It is a matter of speculation whether modern police methods could have achieved a definite identification and conviction of Jack the Ripper. Recent investigations of serial killings have not always been successful or quick: nearly 100 years after the Whitechapel murders, Peter Sutcliffe, the Yorkshire Ripper, remained free to commit further murders after being questioned by police more than once during a very intensive enquiry. It might even be argued that their Victorian predecessors showed better judgement than the modern police force in almost immediately dismissing the Ripper hoaxes as time-wasting nonsense, whereas in the Yorkshire enquiry the police were distracted by a viciously mischievous misdirection. Had fingerprint technology not been in its infancy, the print on the 'saucy Jacky' card might have proved useful—though it would probably have led only to one of the letter writers. DNA evidence might also have led to identification of some of the hoaxers, but might have been useless at leading to the killer unless he really did write some of the letters or left traces at the scenes.

It is a truism that serial killers are notoriously difficult to catch because of the random nature of the crimes and the victims, who are usually strangers to the murderer and to each other. Successful arrests have often resulted from pure chance —blocked drains in the case of Dennis Nilsen, or a clumsily forged will in the case of Harold Shipman. Despite this difficulty, and the 119 years that have elapsed since that dreadful four months in 1888 in Whitechapel, speculation about the true identity of Jack the Ripper has never ceased. There is an unending hope that one day something new just might emerge which will finally lead to the truth.

CHAPTER FIVE

The Ripper Legend

A killer addicted to gory mutilation, an avalanche of threatening letters, victims culled from the 'unfortunate' class, the murky atmosphere of late night Victorian London slums—and a mysterious name. It all makes a potent mix! Yet serial killers are not uncommon, and many unsolved murders lie festering in police files. So what is it about the Ripper murders, horrific and sensational though they were, that continues to fascinate researchers and would-be detectives to this day?

Partly it is that no one was ever caught or punished for the murders. If the Ripper's real identity was known, if he had been unmasked and executed, his deeds would be just another statistic in the annals of Victorian crime. Partly it is that he had a name—albeit a nickname conferred on him by the early letter writers. Partly it is because of the fervid press coverage at the time, and the myths that the reportage created around this sad, vicious woman-slayer—the first serial killer to impinge on modern consciousness. And partly too it is because of the documentation publicly available, which not only allows researchers to examine evidence at first hand and therefore accept the intellectual challenge of trying to solve the case's riddles, but also introduces a 'tingle factor' into the research itself. Handling the original of the 'Dear Boss' letter—albeit now encased in its conserving plastic cover—is an undoubted thrill.

New theories can still be advanced and debated, new material periodically emerges, and the murders are recent enough to allow the hope that perhaps they can be solved. All this helps to explain the Ripper bandwagon.

Meanwhile there are the questions that continue to intrigue and beguile. How many women did the Ripper actually murder? Was Mary Ann Nichols the first and Mary Jane Kelly the last, or were there others before or after? Was Elizabeth Stride a true Ripper victim? Was it really Kelly lying ripped apart in that room, given that witnesses claimed to have seen her alive and well on the morning after her (apparent) death? Was the kidney sent to George Lusk really taken from Catherine Eddowes' body? Who wrote the 'Dear Boss' letter and thereby coined the name 'Jack the Ripper'? Was he the same man who wrote the 'saucy Jacky' postcard? And was it the murderer who wrote the Goulston Street inscription?

Then, apart from the obvious one of his identity, there are the many questions about the killer himself. Was he a man with some medical expertise or knowledge of butchery? Did he have some connection with America? How, exactly, did he set about the murders, given the speed with which some of them were committed?

THEORIES PAST AND PRESENT

Some of these questions will never be answered, but with the advantages of hindsight and of modern forensic and psychological knowledge we are able to make educated assumptions about some aspects of the crimes.

We now almost certainly know how the Ripper set about his work. In the gloom of an East End street he picked out a lone woman, a prostitute willing to lift her skirts for sex in exchange for a few pence. He took her to a dark corner and then against a wall, while her hands were busy with her clothing, he seized her by the throat and strangled her. He then quite gently laid her on the ground (there were no bruises to the back of the head on any of the victims) and proceeded to cut her throat—the wound that killed her—before going on to cut other parts of her body. The mutilations seem to have got steadily worse as the number of his victims mounted: Nichols' abdomen was considerably cut about, two of the next three were disembowelled and the last victim was viciously butchered. It could even be that the Ripper deliberately chose Mary Jane Kelly as his final victim once he knew that she had a room to which she could take him, so that he would have time and privacy for his onslaught on her dead body.

More details of his method can be deduced from the position in which the victims were found. They were usually lying with their left sides against the wall, so the killer was operating from the woman's right side, reaching across her prone body to cut her throat from right to left, thus making it less likely that he would be splashed with blood. He then lifted her clothes and sometimes pushed up her legs to gain access to her abdomen to carry out his other mutilations. In his later murders he took a trophy: a piece of the victim's innards. And he was certainly practised and ready with a knife, whether or not he had knowledge of anatomy. It was the superficial nature of the cuts on Alice McKenzie's body that led one police surgeon to be sure that her murderer was not the Ripper, but perhaps a copycat killer.

The strangling theory is given weight by the medical evidence in three of the cases (Nichols, Chapman and Stride); the other two (Eddowes and Kelly) were so cut around the face that any bruising resulting from finger pressure would probably have been obscured. The evidence in the Chapman case was particularly clear. George Baxter Phillips, divisional surgeon of police, expressed the firm view that the victim had been asphyxiated before her throat was cut (see p. 35). Henry Llewellyn, the doctor in the Mary Ann Nichols case, similarly reported that

> On the right side of the face there is a bruise running along the lower part of the jaw. It might have been caused by a blow with the fist or pressure by the thumb. On the left side of the face there was a circular bruise, which also might have been done by the pressure of the fingers.

There were bruises too on Stride's neck and shoulders, and it seems probable that the aim of the strangling was to make the victim quickly insensible so that she could not cry out. The killing was to be the work of his knife.

So much for the Ripper's method: what about the extent of his activities? Doubts about the tally of true Ripper killings arise from the apparent epidemic of 'Whitechapel murders' occurring at the time. Eleven women were killed between April 1888 and February 1891 and no one was apprehended for any of the crimes. But the belief has always been that the five victims who met their deaths between August and November 1888—Nichols, Chapman, Stride, Eddowes and Kelly—were his prey, with a question mark over the earlier killing of Martha Tabram. The other deaths differed in approach and method, sometimes fundamentally, sometimes more superficially.

Even within the five or six, as we have seen, there are doubts about two of the cases, those of Tabram and Stride. The fact that Stride's body was not mutilated might argue for another hand in this case. However, the vicious nature of the cut to her throat and the clear evidence that she died just before she was found have persuaded most of today's Ripperologists to agree with the police of the time: that the Ripper was responsible, but was disturbed before he could carry out his usual mutilations.

Martha Tabram is a different case. She had been with a soldier that night, she was stabbed with knives which may have included a military weapon, she was killed indoors, unlike most of the other victims, and she was not disembowelled. However, it is arguable that the 39 stabs she suffered were the work of a knifeman at the beginning of his killing spree. Tabram may have been the first to provide the Ripper with the thrill of the chase, the catch, the killing—and the getting away with it. And Mary Jane Kelly may have been the apogee of his blood lust, at which point he could take his obsessions no more and so killed himself or otherwise chose to disappear.

There are theories too about the early Ripper correspondence, again echoed in police speculation at the time. The original 'Dear Boss' letter, dated 25 September, was sent not to the police but to the Central News Agency, as was the 'saucy Jacky' postcard dated 1 October. There are similarities between the handwriting of these missives, and both betrayed intimate—and immediate—knowledge of the details of the crimes. The postcard foretold news of a 'double event' after the first victim 'squealed a bit', and repeated the promise to 'clip the lady's ears'. The writer of the postcard also clearly knew about the letter, as he thanked the police for keeping quiet about it. If the writer of one or both of these missives was not the murderer, he was someone very close to the case, and someone who had immediate access to all the details.

Who else, perhaps, but a journalist—and one working at the Central News Agency? The police clearly believed this to be the case, and it emerged from later material that their suspect was a Tom Bulling, possibly acting with the connivance of his boss John Moore. Robert Anderson's memoirs did not name Bulling, though they claimed that he and other policemen knew the writer and that he was 'an enterprising London journalist'.

Macnaghten confirmed this theory in his memoirs; but it was the Littlechild letter that finally named Bulling—and the identification is given weight by the fact that a third Ripper letter sent by Bulling to the police was in transcript only, although he did send its envelope. It was odd that he did not send the letter itself, but possibly he feared too many connections being made between all three letters and himself. Whether or not the correspondence started as a joke, the Central News Agency benefited from their close connection to the case, as did the press generally.

Other questions surround the witnesses who swore that they had seen Mary Jane Kelly in the street on the morning of her death. There are theories that the victim was not Kelly at all but another woman who had access to Kelly's room while she was out, and was murdered in her place. Some have even speculated that Kelly herself was the murderer, perhaps in cahoots with her lover, Joseph Barnett; others suggest that she took the opportunity to assume the dead woman's identity and clothing and remove herself from Whitechapel, where she was in a lot of debt and had fallen into a miserable way of life. If Joseph Barnett was her accomplice, he would of course have identified the body as hers. If he was not, then the facial injuries might have obscured her features badly enough to convince him that the dead woman was Kelly. And her sickness in the street might have been evidence of a stomach turned by horrors rather than excessive drinking.

A typical hindsight theory perhaps; these are inevitable given that fascination with the murders never ceased. For example, George Sims, 'Dagonet', carried on writing about the Ripper in the *Sunday Referee* for many years afterwards. He frequently repeated his own story that he was the man identified by a stallholder as the customer with bloodied cuffs who had bought a cup of coffee on the morning of one of the murders; the witness had later seen Sims' portrait on one of his books and had taken it to the police.

Another example of the case's long reach occurred in 1949, when a London play on the Ripper caused someone to write to the theatre claiming to be the 84-year-old killer. A newspaper published the signature and compared it with that on the original 'Boss' correspondence, coming to the conclusion that—allowing for the passage of 60 years—the two letters could have been written by the same man. Ripper or not, this man may perhaps have been the writer of the 'Dear Boss' letter—if it wasn't Bulling!

On top of the theories, 'Ripperology' down the years has come up with invention. It is now generally believed that the late Ripper expert Donald McCormick was not above making up some of the stories that formed the basis of his writings on the Ripper, and the confession in the Maybrick diaries is generally regarded as a recent hoax. Indeed it sometimes seems that the odder the theory the more attractive it is. The excellent Ripper website, *Casebook: Jack the Ripper*, runs a poll ranking

the suspects in order of popularity: of all the suspects named by
the police at the time, Francis Tumblety at number two is the
only one to make it into the top four. Maybrick is in first place,
and at third and fourth are two theories involving the artist
Walter Sickert.

The novelist Patricia Cornwell recently announced 'case
closed' in her 2002 book *Portrait of a Killer*. Sickert—number
three in the *Casebook* poll—is her firm suspect, not only as Jack
the Ripper himself but also as the writer of most, if not all, of
the Ripper letters. According to her theory he killed prostitutes
because of a violent hatred of women arising from an anatomical deformity which prevented him from having normal sex.
Her evidence comes from DNA profiles—mostly incomplete—
taken from the Ripper letters, including the Openshaw letter,
as well as material associated with Sickert, though she admits
that there is no full DNA profile available for the painter. She
also produces evidence that many of the letters used artists'
materials or could otherwise be linked with someone of an artis-
tic disposition, and argues that the Ripper systematically set
out to fool the police by writing in a variety of styles and hands.

In fourth place comes the 'royal conspiracy', which also
involved Sickert. Described in Stephen Knight's *Jack the
Ripper: The Final Solution* (1976), it involved a complex cover-
up designed to hide the fact that the Duke of Clarence, Prince
Eddy, had taken to slumming in the East End with Sickert's
connivance, and had sired an illegitimate daughter there.

Ordered by the queen to deal with this embarrassment, the Prime Minister, Lord Salisbury, enlisted the help of her doctor Sir William Gull, who spirited away the woman concerned and removed Eddy from the scene. The woman employed to help look after the baby girl was Mary Jane Kelly, who then gossiped about the prince and the affair to her friends Mary Ann Nichols, Elizabeth Stride and Annie Chapman. So Gull set out to silence them all, assisted by John Netley, Eddy's driver on his slumming trips, and none other than Robert Anderson, the police 'mole' in the operation. The women were murdered by a vicious killer created for the job by the conspirators. Catherine Eddowes, sometimes known as Mary Kelly, was killed because she was the victim of mistaken identity. Walter Sickert later went on to marry the illegitimate daughter, and produced a son, Joseph, who was the source for the story. Knight's book, however, replaced Anderson as a killer in the conspiracy with Sickert himself.

LONDON LIVES ILLUMINATED

It is understandable that much of the fascination with the Ripper case rests on the killer himself—who he was, how he operated, how he got away with it. Yet the story is peopled by others too—the victims, their friends and families, the witnesses, the policemen. They emerge, however briefly, as personalities in their own right from the police evidence or from the press forays into their world. Victorian London, for better or worse, is illuminated by these lives.

As we have seen, the detail given in the newspaper reports paints an extraordinarily rich picture of a place and its people. The *Star* of 1 October, the day after the 'double event', carried over 18,000 words of description, speculation and background. The reporter had left Bishopsgate police station just after 8 am and spent the day wandering round Whitechapel, talking to people in the streets and lodging houses, following up rumours and whispers, sketching in the lives led by the victims and those who knew them. He tracked down the heroine of the hour, a woman known as 'One-armed Liz' from a lodging house in Flower and Dean Street, who had just been to the mortuary to identify Elizabeth Stride's body as that of her fellow resident. Liz was holding court at the house itself:

> On the benches and tables sat or squatted some half a hundred of men and women of all ages and degrees of poverty. A huge fireplace at the end of the room held a cooking apparatus, on which were displayed a score of suppers in course of preparation. And there, in a halo of vile vapour and amid an incense of fried fish stood 'One-armed Liz'. She had the air of a queen as she bowed in deference to the greeting of the scribe…

Liz graciously accepted the *Star* reporter's offer of the price of a bed for the night in return for talking to him, as did a man in the street called Toby who was eager to give a character profile of the murderer: 'It weren't none of the kind that puts up at a sixpenny doss. That chap's got a room to wash himself in. He don't live far off neither. I shouldn't be surprised if he was walking up and down in the crowd out there now. He's a cool one he is.'

As the reporter walked through the streets he was accosted by men whining for the price of a 'doss'. This was a way of life for the Whitechapel residents. As the evidence given at the murder inquests makes clear, these people were willing to turn their hands to almost anything in order to earn a few pence: begging, selling their bodies, and pawning their few possessions when they were really on their uppers—but also buying or making things to hawk on the streets, or going 'hopping' in Kent, as Eddowes had done in the week she died, and as Annie Chapman was prepared to do 'if my sister will send me the boots'. The hard work required in return for a bed and food at the workhouse was to be avoided if possible, but was an option when needed.

The victims, like those around them, were certainly poor and feckless, and all too fond of a drink. But they were also real women who had family, lovers and friends who mourned their deaths. Catherine Eddowes' sister had to stop while giving evidence at the inquest because she was weeping too hard, and there was clearly genuine affection between Eddowes and her common law husband, John Kelly. Her sister confirmed this: she had seen them together a few weeks before her death and described them as 'on happy terms'. Annie Chapman and Elizabeth Stride were described by some who knew them as sober, sensible, respectable women, at least when they were not drunk, and Stride had maintained her contacts with her fellow Swedish exiles in London and so was not friendless.

Mary Ann Nichols may have stolen from her employer, but her father would have given her a home if she had wanted it, because she was 'too good' for the life she was leading; and Mary Jane Kelly had fallen out with Barnett because he had objected to her charitable act in offering another woman a sanctuary in her small room. There was more to these women than the images thrown up by terms like 'prostitute', 'fallen woman' and 'unfortunate'. We know them only through their horrific deaths, but it is possible to imagine them also enjoying the vibrant life of late-Victorian Whitechapel. They may have died in the night-time solitude of the dark, dirty streets, but they lived amid the teeming lodging houses, bright pubs and bustling markets of a real community. On the night she was killed Mary Ann Nichols was rejoicing in her new bonnet; Elizabeth Stride was seen with a flower pinned on her breast, laughing with a man who had his arm round her shoulders; Annie Chapman was enjoying sociable chit-chat in the kitchen of her lodging house; Catherine Eddowes was singing to herself after sobering up in her police cell; and Mary Jane Kelly was also singing songs from her Celtic childhood far into the night. Their murderer is obviously at the centre of the story, but these women have their own vivid reality too. They are more than just his victims.

A PERSONAL VIEW

Without exception, everyone who heard that I was writing this book asked, 'Who do you think he was?' Although my answer was always 'I don't know, and I don't think anyone ever will know for certain,' no one shrugged their shoulders with indifference, or professed ignorance of the crimes and the killer. It would have been surprising if they had, given the continuing fascination with the Ripper murders.

Yet the story goes beyond the killer himself. For me, it is the minutiae of the documentation that fascinates: evidence of how familiar those people were who were caught up in the horrors of 1888—and yet how unfamiliar. We may now marvel at the question posed by the foreman of the jury at Annie Chapman's inquest to the doctor who had carried out her post-mortem: 'Was any photograph of the eyes of the deceased taken, in case they should retain any impression of the murderer?' Dr Phillips' response was noncommittal, and he went on to make a sensible, scientific point about the use of a bloodhound to follow the trail of blood: 'It may be my ignorance, but the blood around was that of the murdered woman, and it would be more likely to be traced than the murderer.' Science and superstition in one small exchange—and evidence of a rapidly changing world.

The surviving documentation is, in truth, relatively scanty, and much of it relates to internal police procedure. Yet it emerges that there were flesh and blood people writing and reading these documents, whose emotions and responses can be read between the lines. The tired frustration of a police officer, and his personal anguish at what he had found; the horror felt by a doctor asked to give all the vile details of a victim's disembowelment to a coroner and his jury; the despair of senior policemen having to report yet another murder—and such a terrible one—to the Home Secretary after weeks of quietude; the testiness of that same Home Secretary with the lack of progress; the sadness of a victim's sister and 'husband' alongside the prurience of mere acquaintances … all of this can be read by those who want to look beyond the grim facts of the Ripper murders.

And then there is the murderer too. If Jack the Ripper had been caught, he would almost certainly have been hanged; the horror of his crimes might well have outweighed even strong evidence of insanity in any argument for a reprieve. Today he would be confined in a mental hospital for the rest of his life— like his successor in prostitute murder, Peter Sutcliffe, the Yorkshire Ripper—and his history and crimes would provide valuable material for research into mental illness. This was a man tormented by terrible urges, driven wild by hatred of women, probably miserable and lonely in his private life. If, as seems likely, he committed suicide after the frenzied mutilations he inflicted on Mary Jane Kelly, what horrors of self-loathing he must have endured and what a desperate, solitary death his too must have been.

Sources & Reading

The original material cited here comes from Metropolitan Police and Home Office documents held by the National Archives, which can be read on microfilm at Kew. See *www.nationalarchives.gov.uk* for visiting information. A research guide giving details of all the files, *Jack the Ripper: The Whitechapel Murders*, is available via the website. The files on the Eddowes murder were among the City of London Police records destroyed during the Second World War, but a few survive as copies within the Home Office records.

The main files are: MEPO 3/140 and 3/141: records of the police investigation; MEPO 3/142, 3/3153 and 3/3157: originals and copies of many of the hoax letters; HO 144/221/A49301C: further police and Home Office reports and correspondence on the cases, including some relating to the City Police investigation of the Eddowes murder; this file also contains copies of the press reports on the inquests. Other Home Office files (HO 144/220/A49301A–B and HO 144/221/A49301D–K) contain peripheral material.

The Corporation of London Record Office and the London Metropolitan Archives also hold Ripper material, including coroners' records and some Ripper letters.

A number of websites deal with the Ripper murders, but by far the best and most comprehensive is *www.casebook.org*.

The National Archives' research guide includes a lengthy list of published books; a few are given overleaf.

P. Begg, *Jack the Ripper – The Uncensored Facts* (Robson Books, 1988)

P. Begg, K. Skinner and M. Fido, *The Jack the Ripper A–Z* (Headline, 1991)

N. Connell and S.P. Evans, *The Man who Hunted Jack the Ripper* (Rupert Books, 2000)

P. Cornwell, *Portrait of a Killer: Jack the Ripper – Case Closed* (Little, Brown, 2002; Time Warner Paperbacks, 2003)

S.P. Evans and P. Gainey, *Jack the Ripper: First American Serial Killer* (Arrow, 1996)

S.P. Evans and K. Skinner, *The Ultimate Jack the Ripper Source-book* (Robinson, 2000)

S.P. Evans and K. Skinner, *Jack the Ripper: Letters from Hell* (Sutton, 2001)

S.P. Evans and K. Skinner, *Jack the Ripper and the Whitechapel Murders* (Public Record Office, 2002)

M. Fido, *The Crimes, Detection and Death of Jack the Ripper* (Weidenfeld & Nicolson, 1987)

M. Harris, *Jack the Ripper – The Bloody Truth* (Columbus Books, 1987)

M. Harris, *The True Face of Jack the Ripper* (Michael O'Mara, 1994)

M. Howells and K. Skinner, *The Ripper Legacy* (Sidgwick & Jackson, 1987)

A. Kelly and D. Sharp, *Jack the Ripper: A Bibliography and Review of the Literature* (Association of Assistant Librarians and Remploy, 1995)

S. Knight, *Jack the Ripper: The Final Solution* (Harrap, 1976)

D. McCormick, *The Identity of Jack the Ripper* (Jarrolds, 1959)

A. Moss and K. Skinner, *The Scotland Yard Files: Milestones in Crime Detection* (The National Archives, 2006)

D. Rumbelow, *The Complete Jack the Ripper* (W. H. Allen, 1975)

P. Sugden, *The Complete History of Jack the Ripper* (Robinson, 1994)

R. Whittington-Egan, *A Casebook on Jack the Ripper* (Wildy, 1975)

PICTURE ACKNOWLEDGEMENTS

Pictures can be seen at the National Archives unless another source is given here. **1, 2, 6, 11, 17, 21, 22** Evans Skinner Crime Archive **4, 25** Mary Evans/David Lewis Hodgson **9** Mary Evans Picture Library **24** Mirrorpix

Index

Numbers in *italic* refer to plate numbers.

Abberline, Frederick George *6, 7, 23,* 28, 37, 41, 45, 69, 76, 85, 89, 90

Anderson, Robert 28, 57, 72, 88, 99, 103

Barnett, Joseph 67–8, 100, 106

Berner Street 43–4

bloodhounds 55–6, 69, 107

Bond, Thomas 66–7, 72–4, 82

Bowyer, Thomas 68

Brodie, William 82

Buck's Row 18, 24, 31

Bulling, Tom 99–100

Bury, William 90

chalked inscription 49–51

Chapman, Annie *4, 5, 7,* 6, 7, 12, 15, 32–41, 75, 97, 98, 103, 105–6

Chapman, George (Severin Klosowski) *24,* 89, 90

Clarence, Duke of (Prince Eddy) 16, 91, 102–3

Coles, Frances 83–4

Connolly, Mary Ann 22–3

Conway (Quinn), Thomas 63

Cox, Mary Ann 68–9

Cream, Neill 91

Cutbush, Thomas 86, 87–8

Davis, John 32–3, 34

'Dear Boss' letter *8,* 8, 9, 42–3, 51, 54, 59, 78, 99, 101

Deeming, Frederick 90–1

Diemshutz, Louis 43

Dorset Street 65–6

Druitt, Montague J. *25,* 87–8, 89

Eddowes, Catherine (Mary Kelly) *9,* 7,

11–12, 46–50, 53, 54, 61–2, 79–80, 83, 89, 95, 98, 103, 105, 106

George Yard 21

Gull, Sir William 103

Hanbury Street *4,* 6, 15, 32–3, 38–9

hoax letters *13, 14,19,* 5, 8, 9, 41–3, 51–2, 54, 58–62, 78–9, 89–90, 92, 93, 99–100, 101

Hutchinson, George *23,* 75–7

Isenschmid, Joseph *7,* 40

Jewish community 49–50

Kelly, John 11–12, 105

Kelly, Mary Jane *21,* 7, 10–11, 65–71, 72, 75–7, 81, 95, 96, 98, 99, 100, 103, 106

Kosminski, Aaron 87–9

Lawende, Joseph 47, 89

'Littlechild letter' 89–90, 100

Llewellyn, Henry 20,
25–6, 97

Long, Elizabeth 34, 75,
104

Lusk, George *17*, 55;
letter to 8, 9, 60–2

Macnaghten, Melville
85, 92, 100; memorandum 86–8

Matthews, Henry 55,
63–4, 72, 85

Maybrick, James 91,
101, 102

McKenzie, Alice 82, 97

McWilliam, James 50,
62–3

method 96–8

Mitre Square 46–8

Monk, Mary Ann
27–8

Monro, James 83, 85

mutilations 7–8, 18–19,
25–6, 31, 34–5, 47, 48,
54, 66–7, 70, 74, 82,
86, 96

Mylett, Rose 81–2

Nichols, Mary Ann *2*,
3, *7*, 7, 11, 18–20, 21,
23–8, 31, 32, 37, 95,
96, 97, 98, 103, 106

Openshaw, Thomas
61; letter to *18*, 9, 62

Ostrog, Michael 87–8

Palmer, Amelia 12,
36–7

pardon 70–1

Phillips, George Baxter
35–6, 82, 97, 107

Pizer, John ('Leather
Apron') 29, 37–8, 85

police 28, 48, 57, 58,
71–2, 84–90, 92–3

press 6, 10, 20, 29–31,
38–9, 53–4, 63, 71–2,
79–81

rewards 55

Richardson, Amelia 15,
33

'royal conspiracy'
102–3

Sadler, Thomas 83–4

'saucy Jacky' postcard
13, 51–2, 54, 93, 99

Schwartz, Israel 44–5,
75, 89

Sickert, Walter 102–3

Sims, George
('Dagonet') 89, 101

slaughtermen 28–9

slum life 10–17

Smith, Emma 20–1, 30,
52, 77–8

Spratling, Inspector *3*,
18–19, 25

strangling 26, 35, 96,
97

Stride, Elizabeth *10*, 7,
16, 43-6, 49, 53, 75,
89, 95, 97, 98, 103,
104, 105–6

suspects 28–9, 56–7,
88–93, 100–3

Swanson, Donald 11,
12, 28, 44, 57, 61, 85,
88, 92

Tabram, Martha 13,
15, 20, 21–3, 31, 81,
98–9

Thicke, John 37, 38, 40,
85–6

Tumblety, Francis
89–90, 102

Walker, Edward 27,
106

Warren, Sir Charles *20*,
41, 50, 55, 57, 59, 65,
70, 72, 84–5

Watkins, Edward 46–7

Whitechapel *1*, 57–8,
103–6; slum life 10–17

Whitechapel Vigilance
Committee 55, 60, 80